A Guide for Tracing and Honoring Your Cherokee Ancestors

CHEROKEE PROUD

by

Tony Mack McClure, Ph.D.

(Julichvyasdi - Awohali)

PUBLISHED BY

CHUNANNEE BOOKS

SOMERVILLE, TENNESSEE

Third Printing

1998

. . . my father is proudly watching his grandson suck his breakfast from his daughter, the baby three quarters Cherokee, more than enough . A few drops of Cherokee blood were required, that was all, to give him a place in the family, full citizenship in the nation, this blood kin of Attacullaculla, the high chief. . .

From "Trail of Tears-The Rise and Fall of the Cherokee Nation." by John Ehle

Respectfully Dedicated to the Memory
of My Great - Grandmother Lucy Briant (Bryant)
A Native American Cherokee
Who Resided at Chu-nan-nee, Old Cherokee Nation, Georgia
Prior to the Trail of Tears . . .

. . . and to the Thousands of Cherokee Men, Women and Children Who Died So Needlessly Along the Paths of that Merciless Journey.

Chunannee Books
4040 Boothe Road, Somerville, TN 38068

Library of Congress Catalog Card Number: 96-95237

ISBN: 0-9655722-1-8

Printed in the U.S.A.

Acknowledgments

Every writing that I undertake involving Cherokee roots and history involves the work of many to whom I must express sincere gratitude. My grandfather Paul McKinley Argo always made sure that I was fully aware of my Cherokee heritage and taught me all that was passed down to him from previous generations. My mother, Marian Argo Haley (Adudalesdi Adawelagisgi), in continuing that tradition, has always gently, but surely, nudged me back to the path of remembrance when I have strayed. For almost 150 years, numerous family members have spent countless hours, days, years, indeed - even small fortunes, to insure that our family archives are as complete and accurate as possible, and I draw from these regularly, regardless of the nature of the work. Among the more recent of these kin: Raleigh Robinson, Betty Robinson, Jere Robinson Cox, Fred Braden , Edith Manor, Lillian Rowe Steele, Ann Tabor, Jean Tabor Benz, Billy Sherrill, Paul Belew, Iva Argo Morales, Beth Argo Beardslee and Brent (Yanusdi) Cox.

To Les Tate, Kate Brantley Alcock (Ayasta), and once again to my cousin Yanusdi, I am deeply grateful for permission to include their excellent published works.

Accolades are due computer gurus Shane Bell and Wayne Carey who kept my machines running smoothly and to my Cherokee sister Sue Morrison who helped keep my sanity intact during this endeavor.

Finally, my wife, Robin McClure (Golanv Adanhdo Unole), deserves special recognition, not only for her assistance, support and understanding, but especially for condoning my profusion of temperamental moods and general neglect.

Table of Contents

Introduction

There is an internal view, a geography of the conscience and soul; we search for its delineations throughout our lives. Those who are fortunate enough to find it ease like a gentle breeze over a placid mountain stream, causing only a faint ripple and are - for the most part - contented. For some, the quest is of a contemporary nature - we seek intimate impressions of those living: a spouse; a child; perhaps a lover. For others, it is a search for obscure roots; a knowledge and better perception of our forebears from whose blood we inherited much of who and what we are.

In the world of the Cherokee, this is not always an easy task, but I have been most fortunate in that regard. Since I was a small boy, my mother, my grandfather, and grandmothers and grandfathers before them instilled in each succeeding generation not only a knowledge of our Native American ancestry, but inherent pride in that unique family legacy.

It would be dishonest of me not to say that, with the exception of my mother, Marian Argo Haley, there have been periods when most of my family members have strayed from acknowledging these inherited hallmarks, even to the point of hiding them completely. In times past, mixed-blood Indian descendants would never have been fully accepted into the mainstream of the predominantly white communities where we always lived, regardless of blood quantum. And the desire to be like the majority seemed to always take precedence over honoring the hopes and memories of our beloved ancestors. For the part of my own life when I shared that attitude, I am truly ashamed.

To borrow words from The Honorable Jim Pell, Principal Chief of the Cherokee Tribe of Northeast Alabama in which over 100 members of my family are enrolled:

"There is no such thing as "part-Cherokee." Either you're Cherokee or you're not. It isn't the quantity of Cherokee blood in your veins that is important, but the quality of it . . . your pride in it. I have seen full-bloods who have virtually no idea of the great

legacy entrusted to their care. Yet, I have seen people with as little as 1/500th blood quantum who inspire the spirits of their ancestors because they make being Cherokee a proud part of their everyday life."

I must forewarn you that throughout this work, I occasionally stray from what critical reviewers might consider normal journalistic standards. By sheer necessity of conscience, opinions occasionally emerge which for me are totally unavoidable. In suggesting ways for you to honor your Cherokee forebears, it is impossible not to point out examples of the horrors they suffered, especially when some of their exploiters are still immortalized today as "valiant." In those instances, if it seems that my intentions are to indict, you are quite correct. The deeds speak for themselves - my words serve merely to inform, but I sometimes indulge in saying what I think. Such is a privilege of self-published authors.

Obviously, since you are reading this book, you have a genuine interest in learning about your Cherokee ancestry. I wish you the best in that endeavor, because if the pursuit is successful, you'll have the extreme pleasure of realizing just what it means to be *Cherokee Proud!*

Tony Mack McClure, Ph.D.

Somerville, Tennessee, November, 1996.

DID YOU KNOW?

On Dec. 29, 1829, the Legislature of Georgia passed an act appropriating a large part of the Cherokee Nation, incorporating it into the territory of their state. It extended the laws of Georgia over this section of the Cherokee Nation and provided that all laws, ordinances or regulations enacted by the government of the Cherokee Nation should be null and void, and made it illegal for any person to justify under any tribal laws. Mississippi and Alabama did the same. The state of Georgia further enacted that any member who sought to influence another not to emigrate to the West should be punished by imprisonment in jail or the penitentiary. It also provided **" that no Indian or descendant of an Indian residing within the Creek or Cherokee Nations of Indians shall be deemed a competent witness in any court of this state to which a white person may be a party."** Governor George Gilmer added an edict giving notice that all Cherokee lands including gold mines belonged to the state and warned Indians and anyone engaged with their consent to cease operating the mines under penalty of Georgia law.

U.S. Senate Document No 512, Vol. II, Twenty-third Congress, first session, "Indian Removal"

Was Your Grandmother Really a Cherokee Princess?

Airings of such popular and colorful Native American movies as *Dances with Wolves, Lakota Woman,* and *Crazy Horse* always seem to inspire a rush of new interest in Native American genealogy circles. I've seen this phenomenon often, and each time questions to my family increase dramatically from people who know us as mixed- blood Cherokee descendants. I'm always happy to take the time to assist people who have a genuine interest in *Tsalagi* culture, but I have to admit I get somewhat tired of hearing that hilarious old axiom "*My great- grandmother was a Cherokee Princess.*"

While there are literally millions of Americans who do have Indian blood, it seems that virtually everyone who wears shoes has been told at one time or another that their great-grandparents were Cherokee, Chickasaw, Creek or whatever. I must alert you that, in some cases, these are simply myths that have no basis in fact, passed down by family members for whatever reasons. One thing you can be absolutely sure of is that no one's grandmother was a Cherokee "*princess,*" because there has never been any such title in Cherokee culture (at least not since Columbus was discovered on our shores). In fact, it might also surprise you to know there was actually no such thing as a "*chief,*" in Cherokee or other Native American hierarchies. In more recent times, the Indians, themselves, adopted the word "chief" as a designated title, but originally it was a term used by white men to describe *high priests*, *elders* or *head men*. In early Cherokee communities, leaders were primarily known by what would loosely translate to "*head men*" and the title closely approximated what we would know today as a mayor. Europeans may have referred to the "mayor's" daughter or other endeared female as *princess,* but no such adaptation was ever recognized by the Indians.

It is important, however, to stress that you should not become discouraged and give up your search for native roots simply because you have always been told there was an Indian "*princess*" somewhere in your lineage. In your ancestor's view and language, "princess" may have been the best descriptive available to characterize the unique relationship they saw between headmen and their biological or adopted female family members.

Richard Pangburn, well-known and respected author of the popular *Indian Blood* series found in most libraries, was kind enough to point out to me that *"nay-sayers of the princess tradition"* often cause people to feel rebuffed and they immediately abandon their quest for Native American roots. That result is certainly not my intention.

There are many misconceptions that continue to permeate people's understanding of the Cherokee. To most people, the term *Indian* conjures up images of dark complexions, black hair with painted faces, loin cloths or other traditional dress of deerskin, beads and feathers. True, there was a period in history when even the Cherokee fit this stereotype, but there has always been a vast difference between these original Smoky Mountain inhabitants and the plains Indians out west.

For the most part, early Cherokees were woodland hunters and farmers and they began to adopt a variation of white man's dress during the Revolutionary war period. Also, because the vast majority of Cherokees are of mixed blood, only a handful now look anything like plains Indians. The number of enrolled people in both federally and non-federally recognized Cherokee tribes today approximates 180,000 and not more than 8500 can properly be called "full-bloods."Yes, you will still see some dark-skinned Cherokee people with jet black hair, but except for a few distinguishing inherited traits, most look very much like any other average citizen you might encounter on the streets. Mixed -bloods have a tendency to be dark under the eyes and very few (whether dark or light) have the stereotypical high cheek bones of other tribes. Some have blond hair and blue eyes and every other "unexpected" combination of traits you can imagine, but they are Cherokee descendants, nonetheless.

If you either know or sincerely believe that your ancestors were Cherokee, you might wonder if the work necessary to substantiate and document it is worth all the effort. Be assured that the culture still is very much alive, and most who successfully complete the task find it both interesting and culturally rewarding to take an active part in this rich heritage. No one understands this better than my trusted friend and fellow author CJ Adair-Stears of the Western Cherokee Nation. CJ has an admirable way with words and she once said to me, *"the rewards derived from searching for Cherokee roots extend far beyond one's own biological family. New friends that I've met along the way have always strengthened my Cherokee soul, my Cherokee mind, my Cherokee spirit."*

Although I doubt that she has ever had to actually search for her own native genesis (CJ is of homegrown *Adair* stock, one of the oldest and most respected family names in modern Cherokee history), this amiable and benevolent lady has spent the better part of the last twenty years preparing an extensive and authoritative new Cherokee family reference text designed soley to help others recognize their own unique origins. The future release of her definitive work "*Cherokee Trails*" will be a highlight for me personally, not only because she is my Cherokee sister, but because I know it will be of great value to everyone involved in *Tsalagi* genealogical exploration.

From a purely personal and impassioned standpoint, it is very important to insure that the Cherokee people never perish from this land where our dead lay buried. The downright savagery inflicted upon the indigenous native peoples of Tennessee, Georgia, Alabama, North Carolina, and other southeastern states deserves to be remembered and fully understood if we are to insure that atrocities like the infamous *Trail of Tears* never happen again.

It has always been my family's view that our ancestors who were so directly and pitifully affected by these actions deserve to be perpetually honored for their sacrifices. Making this proud heritage an important part of our daily lives is how we accomplish this venerable task and helping you to do the same is what this little book is all about.

The Search Begins

There are many places to look for Cherokee ancestors. The best place to begin is at home, talking to your parents, the elderly, and friends of the family. Listen carefully to every old story, regardless of how ridiculous they may seem and make a written record of every word they have to say. Make a copy of every old family document or photograph that anyone has and watch for notations on these i.e., photographers stamps, handwritten dates, names, places, etc. If there are no documents, don't let this dampen your enthusiasm - it is not unusual. Be sure to attend family reunions and take along plenty of film or videotape, writing materials, and an audio recorder.

Attempt to determine where ancestor(s) lived and approximate dates. Learn about any unusual old customs , habits, distinctive dress or traits that anyone can remember.. The most minuscule bit of information that may seem unimportant at first could later prove to be the key that unlocks the mystery.

Recognize that many of our Native ancestors lived through generations of suppressed pride and persecution, so they found it very difficult to hold on to Native American traditions, especially if they lived in mostly white communities. Don't be surprised if some of your older relatives are not overly excited about exploring the details of that part of your family's genealogy. There can be some heavy memories here, so be sensitive to their feelings.

rching the Cherokee Census Rolls is the Next Step

Originally, Native American Indians were to be included in the vital statistics records of each state when states began to keep records, but because they were spread out in large areas, complete registering was not done for many years.

The original Cherokee Census & Roll records are located in the National Archives, The Fort Worth Federal Record Center, the Oklahoma Historical Society in Oklahoma City and a few other Regional NARC Centers. Most are available on microfilm, but a few are available only to researchers who actually visit the depository. All Bureau of Indian Affairs records are a part of National Archives Record Group 75. Microfilm publication identifiers for each record or roll (all part of Record Group 75) listed throughout this book are shown in parentheses immediately following the listing. Because some contain more than one roll of microfilm which may be of interest, I recommend that you review a copy of *"American Indians: A Select Catalog of National Archives Microfilm Publications"* at your local library or available from the National Archives, 7th and Pennsylvania Ave, Washington D.C. 20408. An alternative publication, *"A Guide to Records in the National Archives Relating to American Indians," (order # W100004)* is available for $25 from the National Archives Book Store. This can be ordered by telephone, toll-free at 1-800-234-8861. Additional information on records available from the National Archives is included throughout this book.

Recognize at the outset that traditional methods of conducting family research do not always work when looking for Native American Indians. Cherokees sometimes took orphans, homeless people, widows or other strays into their home and called them "brother, sister, aunt" etc... even when there was no blood relationship at all. It was also an accepted practice to use the mother's family surname and she is often listed on documents as head of household. To further complicate matters, Indian names generally do not offer a clue as to whether the person is male or female.

Many Native Americans were missed completely when the census rolls were taken because of distance, lack of communication and understanding of the language and customs. Others did not want to admit they were Indian and some simply refused to report because they wanted nothing whatsoever to do with white "authorities."

As very few natives could read or write, names were often recorded like they sounded to the person taking the census. (Bryant could be recorded as Bryan, Briant or Brant). Another obvious problem was that many Native Americans had only one name (such as "Crow"). If you have ever been involved with any traditional genealogical surname searches, imagine tackling that one! Many had given and surnames so different from what the record takers were accustomed to that often they did not understand them, much less know how to precisely record them. They simple wrote down whatever came to mind in such cases. This, coupled with the fact that enrollees sometimes gave an Indian name and at others gave an English name, resulted in the same person appearing on different rolls with a different name.

When researching Indian rolls, you can save time by starting with any "knowns" and working backwards in time from there. First, check the most recent rolls for your parents and grandparents. If you determine that neither were enrolled on these as Cherokee citizens, and you know the birth and death dates of any generation of your great- grandparents, calculate the time frames when they would have been living and check all rolls that cover that period. Keep working backwards through several generations.

To fully understand the significance of the various census rolls, it is necessary to understand why they were taken and this necessitates knowing a bit of history about the movements of various tribal groups. Most rolls were recorded by the U.S. Government to document some payment or other transaction between the government and the tribe.

At one time, the Cherokees were known as the mountaineers of the south. When they first saw the white man (Hernando DeSoto in 1540), their territory included some 135,000 square miles covering parts of eight present-day states: North Carolina, South Carolina, Georgia, Alabama, Tennessee, Kentucky, Virginia and West Virginia.

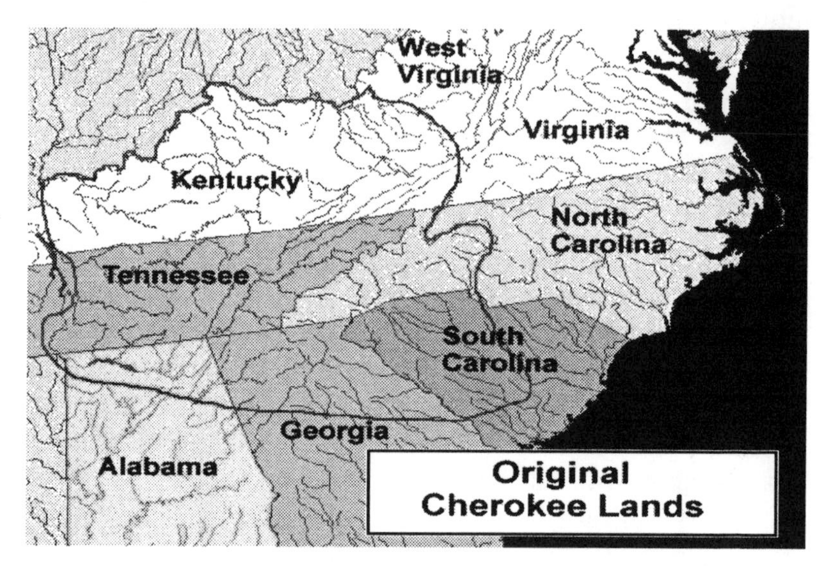

By the end of the American Revolutionary War, the Cherokees had lost over half of their vast land holdings.

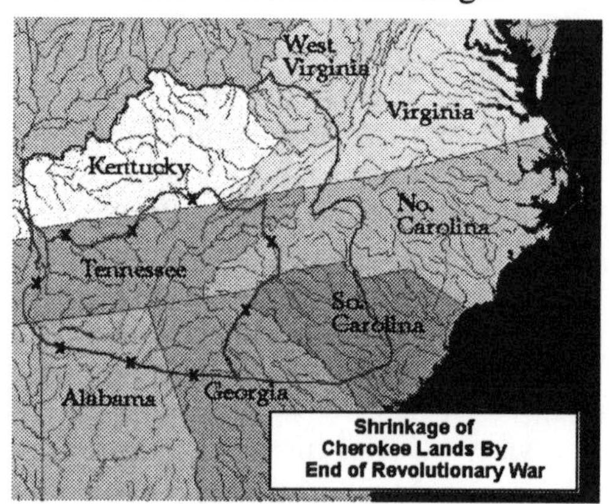

Between 1785 and 1835 the Cherokee lands had shrunk to a few million acres.

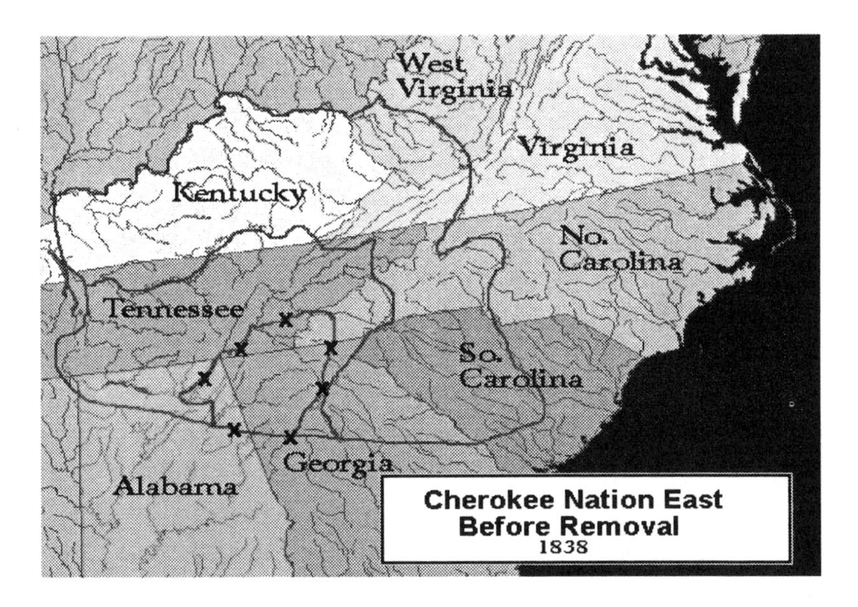

By the "Treaty of New Echota" in 1835, all lands east of the Mississippi River were ceded to the United States Government.

As far back as 1782, a group of Eastern Cherokee who fought with the British in the Revolution petitioned the Spanish for permission to settle west of the Mississippi, which was granted. A group of Eastern Cherokee moved in 1794 into the St. Francis River valley in present-day southeastern Missouri.

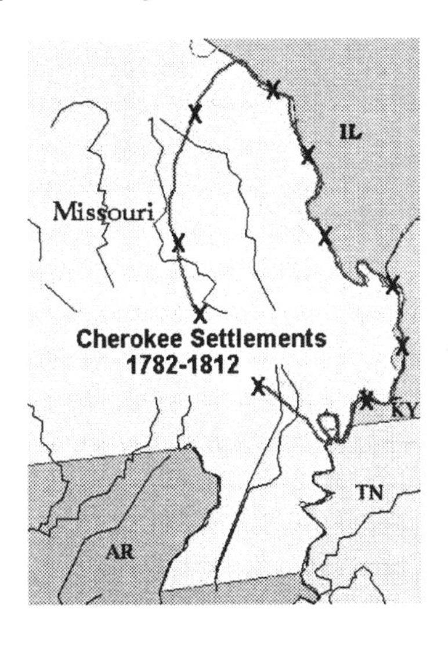

It is probable that there were already Cherokee settled in that area. Records of exactly how many people moved west are limited. Due to the New Madrid earthquakes and flooding in the Missouri bootheel in 1811-12, most of the Cherokee in Missouri moved into present-day northwestern Arkansas. A few remained and the non-federal "Northern Cherokee Nation of the Old Louisiana Purchase" tribe listed later is made up primarily of their descendants.

In the "Turkey Town Treaty of 1817" the Cherokee made a land cession and during the next two years about 1,100 of them removed from their ancestral lands east of the Mississippi to areas in Arkansas Territory. The Cherokee agreed to exchange 1/3rd of their lands in the East for equal acreage located between the White River on the Northeast boundary and the Arkansas River on the Southwest boundary in what was then Arkansas Territory.

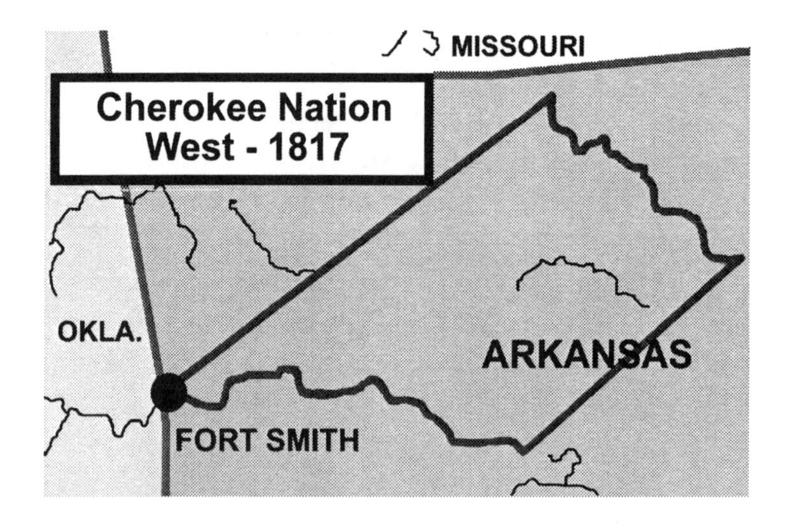

In these "treaties", the Cherokee had a choice of two alternatives: They could either "enroll" to move to the traded land in Arkansas or they could relinquish their Cherokee citizenship and file for a reservation of 640 acres in the east on lands where they already resided. This would revert to the state upon their death or "abandonment" of the property.

The first Cherokee roll you will encounter is known as the ***Reservation Rolls of 1817*** (M-208, and associated records, M-217 and M-218), a listing of those Cherokees desiring the 640 acre tract (mentioned above) in the east and permission to reside there. A total of 311 "heads of households" are listed.

Because this particular roll includes the name of my great-grandmother Lucy Briant, it will be used at this point to illustrate a few of the records my family was able to obtain from the National Archives as a result of making this discovery. This will also demonstrate one of the name spelling discrepancies, mentioned earlier, so often encountered in Indian records.

Grandmother Lucy's name was actually "Bryant" and the certified copy of the original handwritten roll from the National Archives shown on the following page indicates it as such, but later published versions erroneously list it as "Briant."This is also true for some of her other records, and the same variation was noted for two other people on the same roll whose first or last name was either Bryan or Bryant. She was granted reservation plot number 91 known as "*Chunannee*," the land where she was then living, located in what is now known as "Smithgall Woods," a nature conservancy near Helen, Georgia.

This document (page 12) was received from the archives with a note stating *"Original document from Record Group 75 Badly Faded and Torn."* The original had been folded vertically and microscopic examination revealed other important information not readily visible here. The entry to the immediate right of her name in the same column actually says *"A Widow."*A third column to the right (cropped here because it appears only as black when printed) has the entry *"Proxy of B. Rogers."*

A later transcribed version shown on page 14 indicates that when her reservation was assigned in 1817, it was indeed received by one B.R. Rogers as her proxy. Looking again at the top of the roll on page 12, you will note that B.Robert Rogers is the fourth name shown, himself a reservee, in right of his wife.

For over 100 years, members of my family have attempted to determine the relationship between our grandmother and

Page from the Original Cherokee Reservation Roll of 1817 as received from the National Archives

Reservation Roll - 1817

E RESERV

LAST NAME	FIRST NAME	RESERV	LAS
BETTY	LITTLE	RES	C
BIDDY	SHEDRICK	RES	
BIG BEAR		RES	C
BIG BEAR	NANCY	RES	C
BIG GEORGE		RES	C
BIG JACK		RES	C
BIG TOM		RES	C
BIGBY	JAMES	RES	C
BILLEGERS	ANTHONEY	RES	C
BILLEGUS	ANTONIO	RES	C
BIRD	THE	RES	C
BLALOCK	JEFF	RES	C
BLYTHE	WILLIAM	RES	D
BOLD HUNTER		RES	D
BRADY	OWEN	RES	D
BRIANT	LUCY	RES	D
BRISON	SALLY	RES	D
BROWN	ALEXANDER	RES	D
BROWN	JAMES	RES	D
BROWN	JOHN	RES	D
BROWN	JOHN JR	RES	D
BROWN	JOHN SR.	RES	D
BROWN	POLLY	RES	D
BROWN	WILLIAM	RES	D
BRYSON	ANDREW	RES	D
BRYSON	SALLY	RES	D
BUFFALOW		RES	D
BUFFALOW		RES	D
BUFFINGTON		RES	D
BUFFINGTON	CHARLES	RES	

Printed listing of roll page from Bob Blankenship's popular "Cherokee Roots." Note spelling of name as it appears in some National Archives documents.

CHEROKEE BLOOD NEWSLETTER — 16 —

DATE	APPLICATION	NAME	MEMBERS	LOCATION	REMARKS
APRIL 27, 1817	68	SAMUEL RILEY	8	S.SIDE OF TENN.	RIGHT OF WIFE
MAY 1, 1817	69	ANDREW TAYLOR	2	SLICO OLD TOWN	RIGHT OF WIFE
MAY 10, 1817	70	ELI H. HOLT	5	RUNNING WATER TOWN	RIGHT OF WIFE
MAY 10, 1817	71	ROBERT B. VANN	1	NEAR CREEKPATH	NATIVE
MAY 14, 1817	72	JAS. DOHERTY JR	9	HIGHTOWER	"
MAY 14, 1817	73	CHARLES TUCKER	6	HIGHWASSEE RIVER	"
MAY 14, 1817	74	DAVID McELDERTIN	7	HIGHTOWER	"
MAY 14, 1817	75	JAMES DOHARTY SR.	5	HIGHTOWER	"
MAY 14, 1817	76	JOHN MARTIN	2	HIGHTOWER	RIGHT OF WIFE
MAY 14, 1817	77	NANCY GRAVES	2	HIGHTOWER	"
MAY 17, 1817	78	BENJ. TIMPSON	3	HEAD OF HIGHWASSEE	"
MAY 17, 1817	79	SKIWEER	2	TUSQUITTAH	"
MAY 18, 1817	80	ALEX. McDANIEL	11	NOTTLEE	"
MAY 18, 1817	81	THOMAS RAPER	5	TUSQUITAH	"
MAY 18, 1817	82	JESSE RAPER	3	COOSA TOWN	"
MAY 19, 1817	83	SKE LES KEE OR BEAR	8	NOTTLEE	"
MAY 19, 1817	84	CHES QUAH OR BIRD	8	NOTTLEE	"
MAY 19, 1817	85	FERNAHENT	8	NOTTLEE	"
MAY 20, 1817	86	B. ROBERT ROGERS	5	CHU AU TO EE	"
MAY 20, 1817	87	NAKED TURK	"	"	"
MAY 20, 1817	88	JAMES WARD	7	MOUTH OF DEEP CREEK	"
MAY 20, 1817	89	GEO. WARD	6	MOUTH OF DEEP CREEK	"
MAY 20, 1817	90	CATY WARD	3	CHATAHOOCHEE	PROP. OF WM. ENGLAND
MAY 20, 1817	91	LUCY BRIANT	"	"	PROP. OF B.ROGERS
MAY 20, 1817	92	SAMUEL WARD	1	SOQUEE	"
MAY 20, 1817	93	CHARLES WARD	2	DEEP CREEK	"
MAY 20, 1817	94	BRYANT WARD	2	CHATAHOOCHEE	"
MAY 20, 1817	95	ANDR ROBINSON	3	PAINT ROCK CREEK	"
MAY 22, 1817	96	EDWARD ADAIR	5	SOQUEE	"
MAY 22, 1817	97	SAML. ADAIR	5	CHES TA TEE	"
MAY 22, 1817	98	BENJ. COOPER	4	WATERS OF CHATAHOOCHEE	IN RIGHT OF WIFE
MAY 22, 1817	99	REUBIN DANIEL	2	HIGHTOWER RIVER	"
MAY 22, 1817	100	EVAN NICHOLSON	6	SOE QUEE	RIGHT OF WIFE
MAY 22, 1817	101	ANDREW KELLER	8	TOXAU	RIGHT OF WIFE

A Second Version of the 1817 Roll transcribed by the Tennessee State Archives. Note entry of "prop.of" B. Rogers should have read "proxy of".

B.Robert Rogers, but today it remains a mystery.

Perhaps worthy of mention, however - and this serves as a good example of just how much of interest you can learn if you are persistent in your research - we have gleaned more information on Mr. Rogers and others listed on this roll than we ever have on Grandma Lucy. From several records, we learned he was a white man married to a mixed blood Cherokee named Elizabeth "Betsy" Harnage, whom he later abandoned.

Caty Ward, (nee Catherine McDaniel) also listed as "a widow" immediately above Lucy Bryant on this roll was the step daughter-in-law of Nancy Ward, historical, Beloved Woman of the Cherokees. Small world. More on this later.

The printed copy shown on page 13 depicting 1817 roll entries is reproduced from "*Cherokee Roots, Volume 1: Eastern Cherokee Rolls,*" by Bob Blankenship. Note the spelling "Briant," which is not an error on the part of the author, but that of one of the original transcribers obviously spelling the name as it sounded. The transcription shown on page 14 - also using the spelling "Briant," - is from a 1987 Cherokee Blood Newsletter published by the Tennessee State Archives.

Much to her dismay, Grandma Lucy learned the hard way that the "abandonment" rule, mentioned earlier, often was vigorously enforced against reservees who left their property for any extended period, even if they planned to return. National Archive records confirm that around 1826 she left her land in the care of another Cherokee to care for it until she returned from the "west." A few months later, he was dispossessed of the land by a white man under the laws of Georgia.

How do we know all of this? In our case, family information passed down over several generations indicated that our great-grandfather, John Bryant, a Native American Cherokee (son of Lucy Bryant) came from the old Cherokee Nation, Georgia to South Carolina in the early 1800s. From there, he migrated to Lauderdale County, Alabama where he lived for a time, and eventually joined a group of families headed by Davy Crockett, who lived in adjoining Lawrence County, Tennessee, to become one of the early pioneer settlers of Gibson County, Tennessee.

Oral family histories also indicated that grandmother Lucy had lived on reservation land in Georgia in the early 1800's which she later lost. Sometime in the mid to late 1880's, a family member verified that her name was indeed listed on the original 1817 reservation roll shown earlier.

A later generation family member requested any additional information available about Lucy (Briant) Bryant from the National Archives and received the following document which reflects an attempt by her in 1845 to be compensated by the U.S. Government for improvements made to her dispossessed land.

Lucy Briant widow, reservation, Chenanna. May 20, 1818
States that the reservation was taken for her by R. H. Rogers as her proxy, that it embraced the place on which she lived at the time & for eight years afterwards & that she abandoned the reservation when she removed with her son to this country. She was not forced to abandon it. She never sold or made any disposition of it in any way. She left a Cherokee on the place to take charge of it until she returned and he was dispossessed by a white man under the Gov of Georgia. She states she had about 30 acres of cleared land & three small log houses & a stable & crib. The man she left in possession was dispossessed in a few months afterwards, and in about one year after the dispossession she left the Cherokee Nation East and emigrated to the West. She never received any compensation for the improvements, nor is she aware that they were ever valued.

The above statement was made before me this 8th of Feby. 1845

G. W. Washington Comr.

This record reads as follows:

Lucy Briant, widow, reservation Chunannee, May 20, 1818, states that the reservation was taken for her by B.R. Rogers as her proxy, that it embraced the place on which she lived at the time & for eight years afterwards & that she abandoned the reservation when she removed with her son to this country. She was not forced to abandon it. She never sold or made any disposition of it in any way. She left a Cherokee on the place to take charge of it until she returned and he was dispossessed by a white man under the laws of Georgia. She states she had about 30 acres of cleared land & three small log houses & a stable & a crib. The man she left in possession was dispossessed in a few months afterwards and in about one year after the dispossession she left the Cherokee Nation East and emigrated to the West. She never received any compensation for the improvements, nor is she aware that they were ever received.

The above statement was made before me this 8th of July, 1845.

E.C.Washington,
Comm.

Over two years later on July 20, 1847 her claim was rejected as reflected by the simple documents on page 18.

The Cherokee Emigration Rolls of 1817-35 lists Cherokees who voluntarily enrolled themselves as emigrants to the Arkansas country and relinquished all rights, titles and claims to lands within the limits of the Cherokee Nation east of the Mississippi River. This group is also known as the "Old Settlers." It should also be noted that many who put their names on these rolls to go west never actually went. No record exists of the 2,500 or so Cherokees who emigrated to Northwestern Arkansas before 1818 without enrolling.

In 1828, at U.S. Government insistence, the Cherokees ceded their treaty acquired lands in Arkansas for land in Indian Territories (later to become Oklahoma).

1199

Fourth Commission.

Lucy Briant, (Widow
vs: — Reservation 91.
The United States.

Filed with former Board.
W. D. Miller, Secy.

Decree rendered July 20, 1847. rejecting claim.
W. D. Miller, Secy.

Decree Lucy Briant
1199 vs Reservation 91.
The United States.

And now on this day came the claimant, and the Commissioners having fully considered the papers submitted to a former Board - that is to say: 1, statement of claimant - do adjudge and decree that this claim be rejected. The reservation was abandoned as by the admission of the reservee.

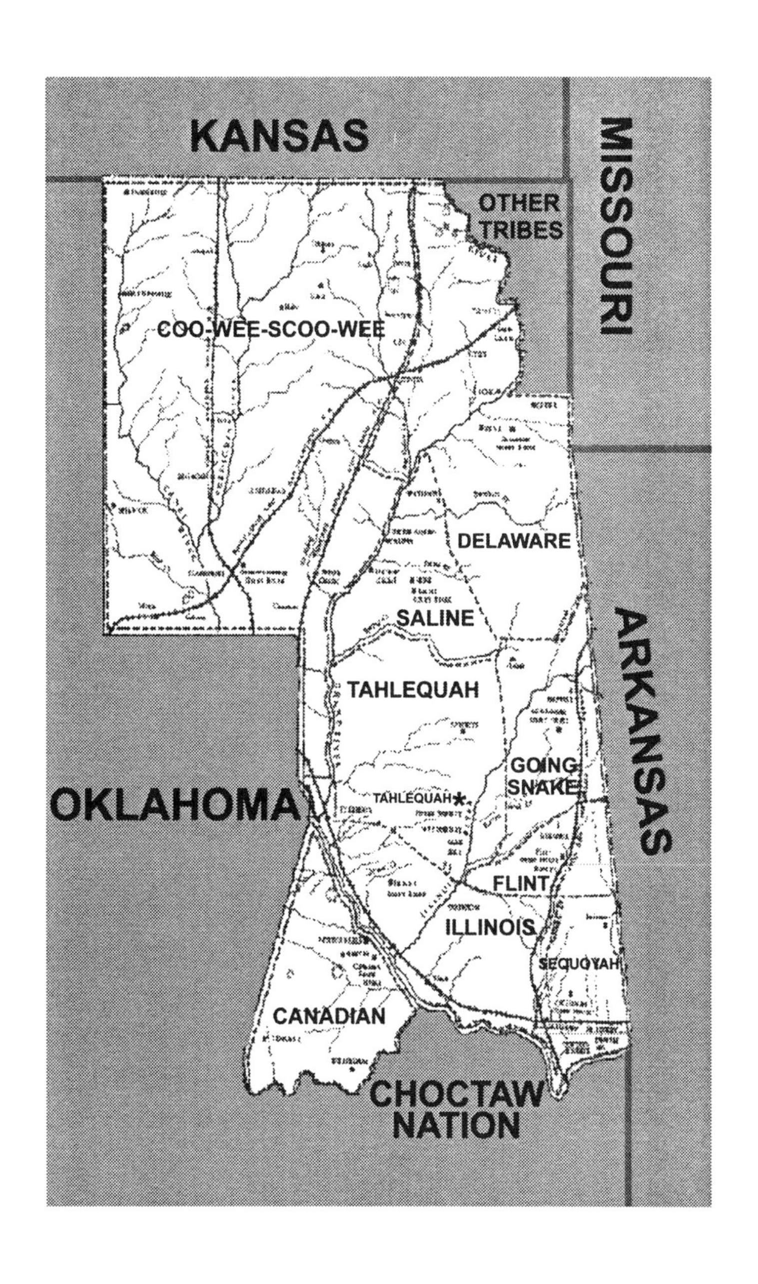

In 1828, the Cherokees ceded their treaty acquired lands in Arkansas for land in Indian Territories (later to become Oklahoma).

The fraudulent *"Treaty of New Echota,"* 29 Dec 1835, represented the final cession of all Cherokee lands east of the Mississippi. A census known as the **Henderson Roll, 1835** (T-496), intended as a final enumeration of Cherokees to be removed to the west, was taken of the Eastern Cherokees before they were forced to move on the infamous " Trail of Tears" to Oklahoma. In the three years between 1835 and 1838, however, no records seem to have been kept of Cherokee Indians who were born, died along the way, (4000 of them), who never left their homes, or who initially reached the new territory in the west. Also, it includes a large number of Cherokees who somehow avoided the removal and omits many who were actually removed. The Commissioner of Indian Affairs in 1835 (a Major Currey), who was in charge of this census, classified as "Indian" anyone with 1/4 degree of Indian blood.

In 1838, several hundred (the figure is thought to be much higher by some scholars) Cherokees in the East escaped into the mountains of North Carolina and later became known as the Eastern Band of Cherokees. Others dispersed to various parts of the country and managed to become assimilated into white communities. At about the same time, many Cherokees elected to take advantage of Article12 of the 1835 treaty which allowed those desiring to stay in the east to do so if they met certain criteria.

The Henderson Roll includes only family heads by name, but records numerous columns of data including residence by state county and watercourse, number of persons in household by age and sex, inter-married whites, racial mix, slaves, whether persons could read English, various agricultural data, including acres cultivated and bushels harvested.

The Mullay Roll of 1848 (#7RA-06) was a listing of 1,517 Cherokees living in North Carolina after the removal of 1838. Agent John C. Mullay took this census pursuant to an act of Congress in 1848.

The Siler Roll of 1851(#7RA-06) is a listing of 1,700 Cherokees living in North Carolina, Tennessee, Georgia and Alabama who were entitled to a per capita payment pursuant to acts of Congress in 1850 and 1851. It is commonly agreed that many Cherokees wanted no part of the payment or any connection with white government officials and simply ignored it. [See sample page on page 22].

The Old Settler Roll, 1851(M-685) lists Cherokees still living in 1851who were already residing in Oklahoma when the main body of the Cherokee arrived in the winter of 1839 (Trail of Tears). Approximately one third were Old Settlers and two thirds were new arrivals. Accordingly, a treaty in 1846 concluded that the old settlers were entitled to one-third of the removal payments authorized in the removal treaty of 1835. This roll is a listing of those receiving these per capita payments. It lists each individual by district with his/her children unless the mother was an emigrant Cherokee. In this case, the children were listed with their mother on the Drennen Roll of 1852, listed below. There were 44 family groups listed as non-residents. [See sample page on page 23] (Note: Guion Miller used this roll in compiling the 1910 record listed later).

The Chapman Roll, 1852 (M-685) prepared by Albert Chapman is a listing of those Cherokee actually receiving payment based on the above Siler 1851 roll. In 1851 and 1852, the per capita payments were made by Chapman based on Silar's census to 2,134 individuals (This roll played an important part in the preparation of the Guion Miller roll completed in 1910. Anyone who could trace their ancestry to an individual on the Chapman Roll was included on the Miller roll) [See sample page on page 24].

Drennen Roll 1852. (M-685) prepared by John Drennen as a first Census of the "New" arrivals of 1839 to Oklahoma on the Trail of Tears. It contains the names of 14,094 individuals who received a payment of $92.83 made to those living in the west who came there as a result of the 1835 treaty. A section of it, known as the "Disputed Roll," lists 273 individuals who emigrated west before

No 22 87

No.	Name	Age	Relation	Sex		Remarks
1935	Thomson Lingard	49		M	white	
1936	Jane Lingard	20	D	F	mixed	
1937	Andrew Lingard	18	"	M	"	

Union County Georgia

No 1

No.	Name	Age	Relation	Sex		Remarks
1938	Mary Ann Sneed	22	wife	F	mixed	A. L. Sneed is head of this family—
1939	John H. Sneed	4	S.	M	"	
1940	Sarah E. Sneed	2	D	F	"	

No 2

No.	Name	Age	Relation	Sex		Remarks
1941	James Blythe	46		M	White	
1942	Sally Blythe	46	wife	F	mixed	

No 3

No.	Name	Age	Relation	Sex		Remarks
1943	Macy Beck	25	wife	F	mixed	Berry Beck is head of this family
1944	James Beck	1	son	M	"	

No 4

No.	Name	Age	Relation	Sex		Remarks
1945	Elizabeth Meadows	23	wife	F	mixed	
1946	Sarah Meadows	3	D	"	"	
1947	Mary J. Meadows	1	"	"	"	

No 5

No.	Name	Age	Relation	Sex		Remarks
1948	Caleb Cope Thompson	20		M	mixed	
~~1949~~	~~William Thompson~~	~~1~~	~~son~~	~~M~~	~~"~~	

No 6

No.	Name	Age	Relation	Sex		Remarks
1950	Mary Ward	40		F	white	
1951	Sarah Ward	21	D	"	mixed	
1952	Vanvert Ward	18	"	"	"	
1953	Amanda M Ward	14	"	"	"	
1954	Cherokee Ward	13	"	"	"	
1955	Martin Ward	12	S	M	"	
1956	Samuel F. Ward	10	"	"	"	

Sample Page from the Siler Roll of 1851

CHEROKEE OLD SETTLER PAY ROLL.

ROLL OF 1851.	CARD NO.	O.S. NO.	AGENCY PAY NO.	NAMES.	AGE.	SEX.	PER CAPITA.	AMOUNT PAID.	POSTOFFICE ADDRESS.	SIGNATURES.	DATE OF RECEIPT.
				Amount brought forward.							
G.S. 11	223	7	1	George W. Ward Jr.	73	M			Siloam Springs Ark		
G.S. 7	439	2	2	Rosa Dittle	70	F			Vinita		
G.S. 7	440	3	3	James M. Dittle	47	M			Vinita		
G.S. 7	441	4	4	Amelia Sager, nee Dittle	46	F			Grove		
G.S. 7	442	5	5	Robert W. Dittle	45	M			Vinita		
G.S. 11	947	6	6	Lucy Ann Gass nee Ward	48	F			Tahlequah		
[illegible] 32	[illegible]	7	7	Thomas Ward	47	M			Vogel		
G.S. 6	89	8	8	Mary E. Swim nee Ward	43	F			Claremore		

Sample Page from Old Settler Roll, 1851

CHAPMAN

NO.	NAME	AGE	RELATION-SHIP
	HAYWOOD COUNTY.		
	Paint Town.		
1	Ah-yee-kih	26	
2	Ah-lee-kih	24	W.
3	Wal-suh	5	D
4	Sou-wut-chee	3	D
5	Wakee	1	D
6	Au-soo-kil-leh 15790	40	
7	Che-no-kih 15790-1	28	W
8	Ah-kim-nih	5	D
9	Ta-tee-kih	1	S
10	Ah-nee-cheh (Blacksmith) 6765	40	
11	Jinny	24	W
12	Uh-hee-lee	18	D
13	Le-how-wih	15	D
14	Al-seb	5	D
15	Ma-lee or Mary	3	D
16	Wee-lee-wes-tee 9998	1	S
17	Ah-yu-wee or Isaac Davis 1069	42	
18	Doo-ti-yeh	32	W
19	Stacy 1067	13	D
20	Cho-co-he [illegible]	11	D
21	Wee-lee-tee-wee-see	8	S
22	Wee-loo-stee	5	S
23	Tau-nee	[illegible]	D
24	John	[illegible]	S
25	As-stoo-ge-cut-to-keh	27	
26	Ne-chil-leh 9997	28	W
27	Tau-se-ki-ya-kel	[illegible]	S [illegible]
28	Ne-del-line-ih	1	D
29	Ah-yeh-he-neh [illegible]	26	
30	Qua-ke	[illegible]	[illegible]
31	Lucy	[illegible]	D [illegible]

Sample Page from Chapman Roll of 1853

the Treaty of 1835, but returned east before the removal.

Federal Census 1860. (M-653 Rolls 52 & 54) contains Indian lands in Arkansas.

Tompkins Roll 1867. (#7RA-04) An 1866 Treaty required that a census be made of Cherokees residing in the Cherokee Nation. There are also Indices of Freedmen with this roll.

Swetland Roll 1869. Prepared by S.H. Swetland as a listing of those Cherokee and their decedents who were listed as remaining in North Carolina by Mullay in his 1848 Census. An act of Congress in 1868 provided for a removal and subsistence payment.

Federal Census 1880 (T-9) Check Federal Territorial Census rolls using the names and locations found in the Indian Rolls. (Note the 1880 Indian Schedules for this Federal Census were destroyed.)

Roll of Rejected Claimants, 1878-80. Listed by case number, this list includes persons whose applications for citizenship were rejected by the Cherokee Citizenship Commission.

Cherokee Census, 1880 (#7RA-07). In 1879, the Cherokee National Council authorized this census as a list of persons entitled to a per capita payment of $16.55. It is sometimes referred to as the list for "bread money" as the purpose of the payment was for the purchase of "bread stuffs." The census was arranged in 6 schedules, including Cherokee citizens, Adopted whites, Shawnees, Delawares. Freedman, Orphans, Citizenship claimants whose applications were either pending or rejected, Intruders, and Individuals living in the nation under permit. (Note that some information from this roll is missing).There is also a receipt roll (#7RA-33) prepared by the Cherokee Nation treasurer listing persons who actually received this payment.

Commission Docket Book 1880-84 (# 7RA-26). A listing by case number and session of the citizenship committee. Includes individual names , nature of claims and decisions.

Cherokee Seminaries Register, 1881-82. A register of students and boarders at the male and female seminaries by term.

Cherokee Census, 1883 (# 7RA-29). Authorized by the National Council in 1883, this list includes orphans, prisoners and "supplemental roll of citizens."

Receipt Roll, 1883 (#7RA-56 and 57). Prepared for a per capita payment of $15.50 authorized by the National Council.. The list is by enrollment number and district and includes the names of witnesses to the payment as well as the person receiving payment.

Hester Roll, 1883 (M-685) . Prepared by Joseph G. Hester as a listing of Eastern Cherokee in 1883. (This Roll is an excellent source of information. Includes ancestors, Chapman Roll Number, age, English name and Indian name).

Copies of the previous census were made available to Hester and he was required to account for all persons on the previous rolls by either including them on the new roll, noting their deaths on the old rolls or describing their whereabouts as unknown. This completed roll was submitted to the Secretary of Interior in1884. It contained 2,956 persons residing in North Carolina,Tennessee, Georgia, Alabama, South Carolina, Virginia, Illinois, Kansas, Colorado, Kentucky, New Jersey, and California. Those living west of the Mississippi and listed by Mr. Hester were descendants of members of the Eastern Band and had no affiliation with the Cherokee Nation in the west.

Cherokee Census Roll, 1886 (#7RA-58). On July 28, 1897 an act of the Cherokee Council directed this roll be made of persons who received a per capita payment in 1886. It includes the name of the head of household as well as all members of the household, their ages and relationship.

Cherokee Census Roll, 1890 (#7RA-60). Created also in 1897 as a result of the council act listed immediately above. Listings are the same except it goes a step further to include whether each household member was a Cherokee, Delaware, Shawnee, White Person or Freedman.

Cherokee Receipt Roll, 1890 (#7RA-59). Listing of persons who received a per capita payment of $13.70 made by the Cherokee Nation treasurer.

Cherokee Census Roll, 1890 (#7RA-08). This census contains a wealth of information including 6 schedules of status (Indian by type, orphan, rejected claimant, intruder,etc. and 105 columns of information pertaining to each i.e., age, marriage status, whether the person could read or write, and occupation designator - agricultural manufacturing, etc.).

Federal Census 1890.(M-123) Indian Territory. Taken in 1890, this census of the Cherokee Nation is probably the most complete of any of the census. It included Cherokees and adopted whites, Shawnees and Delawares, orphans under 16 yrs, those denied citizenship by the Cherokee authorities, those whose claims to citizenship were pending, intruders and whites living in the Cherokee Nation by permission

Wallace Roll, 1890-93 (Freedmen Roll & Index). This roll was based on an 1883 list taken of freedmen(freed blacks) entitled to a per capita payment authorized in 1888. **It was set aside as fradulent by the U.S. Court of Claims and was never recognized by the Cherokee National Council.**

Cherokee Census Roll, 1893 (#7RA-54). In addition to Cherokee citizens, this list also includes intermarried whites, adopted whites and Creek Indians living in the Cherokee nation.

Starr Roll, 1894 (#7RA-38). Prepared as a receipt roll for each person authorized to receive a per capita "strip payment" of $265.70 for the sale to the United States of over 6 ½ million acres of Cherokee land known as the *Cherokee Strip.*

Cherokee Census Roll 1894. This roll was taken in 1897, but was based on an 1894 payroll.

Cherokee Childrens List, 1895-97. List of Cherokee children born between 1895-97; includes parents name and date of birth.

Cherokee Census Roll, 1896 (#7RA-19). This is the first census which includes any reference to blood degree. Also includes place of birth of enrollees as well as Adopted Whites, Orphans, Asylum Inmates, Colored, Doubtful Citizens, Rejected Persons, Shawnee and Delawares.

Clifton Roll (Cherokee Freedmen), 1896. Prepared by commission appointed by the U.S. Dept. of the Interior, based on testimony taken from May to August, 1897.Includes freedmen and their descendants and a supplemental list of freedmen whose citizenship was rejected by the Cherokees, but approved by the commission.

Old Settler Payment Roll 1896. (T-985) The 1896 Payment Roll is based on the 1851 Old Settler Roll listed earlier and listed each payee's 1851 roll number, name, age, sex, and post office address. This roll can be an important source to determine the descendants of persons listed on the Old Settler rolls and not still living in 1896 when a per capita payment of $159.10 was paid. Their heirs could receive the payment.

Dawes Roll of 1898-1914 (M -1186). On March 3, 1893, the U.S. Congress established a commission to negotiate with the 5 Tribes (Cherokee,Choctaw, Creek, Chickasaw, and Seminole Nations) in Indian Territory, to abolish their tribal governments and to allot their tribal lands to individuals. The head of this commission was U.S. Senator Henry Dawes. The tribes were not in favor of this proposal and were forced to accept it after numerous efforts, including a proposal from the Indian Nations to form their own State, to be called Sequoyah. All of these efforts were ignored, blocked or sabotaged by the U.S. Government.

The U.S. Congress passed the Curtis Act in June 1898 which severely limited the power of tribal governments. It gave the Dawes Commission authority to survey and supervise the allotment of lands, sell unallotted lands, prepare and deliver deeds, and required that a new Indian Roll would be created to supersede all previous rolls. This came to be known as the Dawes Rolls.

The U.S. Government sent census takers into Indian Territory [Oklahoma], to interview tribal members. To be enrolled, citizens had to complete an application (or Government agents interviewed them and filled out the application), then they decided if the person was "qualified" to be on the Roll.

The Dawes commission enrolled tribal citizens under several categories: Citizens by Blood, Citizens by Marriage, New Born Citizens by Blood, Minor Citizens by Blood, Freedmen (former Indian black slaves), New Born Freedmen, and Minor Freedmen.

The Delaware Tribal members adopted by the Cherokee Nation were enrolled as a separate group within the Cherokee Nation records. There are also a few Mississippi Choctaw and some Chickasaw cards that refer to tribal members never finally enrolled.

There is a census card which contains the information provided by individual applicants from the same family group or household. The cards provide notation of the action taken by the Dawes Commission such as rejected, approved, or doubtful. For each applicant, they list name, enrollment number, age, sex, degree of Indian Blood, relationship to head of family, parent's names, and references to enrollment on earlier Rolls (used by the commission for verification of eligibility). Some references to enrollment cards of relatives are noted, as well as notations about births, deaths, changes in marital status, and actions taken by the Commission and the Secretary of the Interior.

It is important to note that the card numbers DO NOT match the Roll numbers. There is an index to the final rolls which provides the Roll number for each person. The actual applications may contain information which is not on the Census card. Researchers should examine both the Census Card and the Application (Applications are contained in Enrollment "Packets" listed below)[See Page 31 for Sample Dawes Census Card].

The Dawes Rolls were U.S. Government tribal enrollment records which were used to enumerate all the Indians in a particular tribe. When everyone was counted, tribal land held in common was taken away, allotments were made to everybody listed on the rolls, then all that was left over was sold to white settlers, railroads, and private companies, usually at an absurd discount.

This was supposed to be a final step in the assimilation of the "*Indian Problem*" within the United States. Many Cherokees refused to enroll and did so only after a federal court order threatened them with imprisonment. Some refused to accept land allotments, even after the enrollment, and were arbitrarily assigned parcels by the government.

Included within the available Archives documents pertaining to the Dawes enrollment proceedings are:

Dawes Commission Enrollment Cards. 1899-1907. Microfilm roll 1 is an index. Rolls 2-38 are Cherokee cards. (Rolls 39-93 contain cards for the other five civilized tribes).

Dawes Commission Enrollment Packets, 1899-1907. Almost all of these contain interviews which contain more information than that on the census cards above. Some have death or marriage certificates, etc. included as supporting evidence.

Final Dawes Rolls of Citizens and Freedmen, 1902-1906. Today, this roll continues to serve as the only basis for determining eligibility for membership in the Cherokee Nation of Oklahoma.

Record of Allotments, 1903-1914. Records of final land allotments by Dawes enrollment number including legal descriptions of the tracts and appraised values.

RESIDENCE: Cooweescoowee DISTRICT.

POST OFFICE: Chelsea, I.T.

Cherokee Nation. Cherokee Roll. 2515

(Not including Delawares, Shawnees, or Freedmen.)

CARD NO.

FIELD NO.

Dawes' Roll No.		NAME	Relationship to Person First Named	AGE	SEX	BLOOD	TRIBAL ENROLLMENT Year	District	No.	TRIBAL ENROLLMENT OF PARENTS Name of Father	Year	District	Name of Mother	Year	District
6398	1	Williams, Elizabeth	Named	30	F	1/2	1880	Cos	801	Jack Downing	Dead	Cos	Rachel Downing	Dead	Cos
6399	2	" Charley	Son	13	M	1/4	1896	"	5031	Henry Williams	"	Non Citz	No 1		
6400	3	" Pearl	Dau	11	F	1/4	1896	"	5032	" "	"	"	No 1		
6401	4	" Hattie M.	"	7	F	1/4	1896	"	5033	" "	"	"	No 1		
6402	5	" Clem	Son	2	M	1/4							No 1		
6403	6	" John	Son	6 mo	M	1/4							No 1		

Citizenship Certificate issued for No 1-2-3-4-5-6 Oct 24 1904

No 1 on 1880 Roll as Lizzie Downing

No 5 affidavit of birth to be supplied

Filed Sept 11, 1900.

No 1 on 1896 Roll Page 278 No 5030 as Lizzie Williams [illegible]

No 6 enrolled Feb 18, 1901

No 1 evidence of marriage of No 1 to W. H. Williams

Filed Feb 18, 1901

OK

See NB# 2468.

Sample Dawes Census Card

The Guion Miller Roll and Applications, 1906 (M-1104 and M-685). On July 1, 1902, the U.S. Congress gave the U.S. Court of Claims jurisdiction over any claim against the United States filed by the Cherokee Tribe, or any band thereof. Three lawsuits were brought against the U.S. Government as grievances from Treaties violation(s).

1.The Cherokee Nation v. the United States, Case # 23199
2.The Eastern & Emigrant Cherokees v. the U.S., Case # 23212
3.The Eastern Cherokee v. the U.S., Case#23214

On May 18, 1905 the U.S. Court of Claims ruled in favor of the Eastern Cherokee and directed the Secretary of the Interior to identify persons entitled to a portion of the money appropriated by the U.S. Congress on June 30, 1906, to be used for payment of the claims. Special Agent Guion Miller, U.S. Dept. of the Interior, began this work and then was appointed by the U.S. Court of Claims as a Court Special Commissioner.

The Court decree specified that the money was to be distributed to all Eastern & Western Cherokees alive on May 28, 1906 who could establish that they were members of the Eastern Cherokee Tribe or descendants of such members. They could not be members of any other tribe. All claims had to be filed prior to August 31, 1907.

In Agent Miller's report of May 28, 1909, he listed 45,847 applications listing approximately 90,000 individual claimants. Among these 30,254 were enrolled and eligible for a share of the funds; 27,051 lived west of the Mississippi River, and another 3,203 lived east of the Mississippi River. The Roll includes information on both accepted and non-accepted members and the individual applications themselves contain a wealth of genealogical data.

Miller used previous census lists and rolls of the Cherokees. These rolls included: the Hester, Chapman, and Drennen Rolls, and other materials from 1835 to 1884, but did not include Old Settler Cherokees.

These records are part of the U.S. National Archives, Record group 75, Records of the Bureau of Indian Affairs, previously mentioned. Other records relating to this enrollment, including the applications themselves, however, are in U.S. National Archives Record Group 123.

Special Commissioner of the Court of Claims,
601 Ouray Building, Washington, D. C.

SIR:

I hereby make application for such share as may be due me of the fund appropriated by the Act of Congress, approved June 30, 1906, in accordance with the decrees of the Court of Claims of May 18, 1905, and May 28, 1906, in favor of the Eastern Cherokees. The evidence of identity is herewith subjoined.

NOTE: Answers to all questions should be short, but complete. If you can not answer, so state.

1. State full name: Callie Murry Belew
   English name: Callie Murry Belew
   Indian name: Bryant was my Indian n
2. Residence and post office: Miami
3. County: Ottawa
4. State: Oklahoma
5. How old are you? 32 Born 1874
6. Where were you born? Gibson County Tennessee
7. Are you married? yes
8. Name and age of wife or husband: Frona Belew age 26 ... 1881
9. To what tribe of Indians does he or she belong? Cherokee
10. Name all your children who were living on May 28, 1906, giving their ages:

	NAME.	AGE.	BORN.
(1)	Bulah Belew	8	nov the 19 1
(2)	Melissa Belew	7	august the 1
(3)	Blanch Belew	4	jun the 28 1
(4)	All Borned in the cherokee nation		
(5)	I have been here for 23 years		
(6)			

11. Give names of your father and mother, and your mother's name before marriage: Geo Belew Sarrann Belew Sarrann Bryant
    Father—English name: Geo Belew # 3298
    Indian name: Geo Belew
    Mother—English name: Sarrann Belew
    Indian name: Sarrann Bryant
    Maiden name: Sarrann Bryant
12. Where were they born?
    Father: west Tennessee Gibson Co
    Mother: west Tennessee Gibson Co

Page 1 of a 3 Page Miller Roll Application

13. Where did they reside in 1851, if living at that time?

Father: West Tennessee Gipson Co

Mother: West Tennessee Gipson Co

14. Date of death of your father and mother:

Father: Still living

Mother: mother died in 1885

15. Were they ever enrolled for money, annuities, land or other benefits? If so, state when and where, and with what tribe of Indians: no

16. Name all your brothers and sisters, giving ages, and residence if possible:

	NAME.	BORN.	DIED.
(1)	Monroe Belew, Miami Okla	1861 Tennessee	Living
(2)	the rest all ded Sisters		
(3)			
(4)			
(5)			
(6)			

17 State English and Indian names of your grandparents on both father's and mother's side, if possible:

FATHER'S SIDE.	MOTHER'S SIDE.
Samuel Belew	Mary Bryant Indian n.
Martin Bryant	Mary Belew english n.
	Mary as Polly Smith the Sc
	Dolly Smith Bryant

18. Where were they born? in South Carolina

19. Where did they reside in 1851, if living at that time? Grand father was dead Grand mother was living in west tennessee

20. Give names of all their children and residence if possible

(1) Hanah Belew
(2) Eliza Belew
(3)
(4) Monroe Belew
(5) Riel Belew
(6) Aron Belew
(7) Martin Belew
(8) Silas Belew
(9) John Belew

(11) Betsy Belew
(12) Cornelia Belew
(13) Jimie Belew
(14) Tennessee Belew
(15) Govones Belew
(1) Judge Bryant
(2) John Bryant
(3) Jim Bryant
(4) Ellen Bryant

6. Amanda Bryant
Jane Bryant
(8) Minnie Bryan
(9) Sarah

Page 2 of a 3 Page Miller Roll Application

21. Have you ever been enrolled for money, annuities, land or other benefits? If so, state when and where, and with what tribe of Indians: *None*

22. To assist in identification, claimant should give the full English and Indian names, if possible, of their parents and grandparents back to 1835: *my Grate Grand father John Bryant was a cherokee indian he moved from south Kalina to tennessee about 1832 [illegible]*

REMARKS.

(Under this head the applicant may give any additional facts which will assist in proving his claim.)

my fathers Brother [illegible] Bryant his [illegible] by proving that Grand father Bryant was a cherokee indian the [illegible] [illegible] [illegible] [illegible]

I solemnly swear that the foregoing statements made by me are true to the best of my knowledge and belief.

(Signature) *Callie Murry Belew*

Subscribed and sworn to before me this *27th* day of *June* 1907.

D. W. Talbot
Notary Public.

My commission expires *May 30th* 1909.

AFFIDAVIT.

(The following affidavit must be sworn to by two or more witnesses who are well acquainted with the applicant.)

Personally appeared before me *J. M. McDaniel* and *William Bledsoe*, who, being duly sworn, on oath depose and say that they are well acquainted with *Callie Murry Belew* who makes the foregoing application and statements, and have known *him* for *8* years and *8* years, respectively, and know *him* to be the identical person *he* represents *himself* to be, and that the statements made by *him* are true, to the best of their knowledge and belief, and they have no interest whatever in *this* claim.

Witnesses to mark.	Signatures of Witnesses.
	J. M. McDaniel
	William Bledsoe

Subscribed and sworn to before me this *27* day of *June*, 1907.

My commission expires *May 30th* 1909. *D. W. Talbot*
Notary Public.

NOTE.—Affidavits should be made, whenever practicable, before a notary public, or clerk of the court, if sworn to before an Indian agent or disbursing agent of the Indian service, it need not be executed before a notary, etc.

Page 3 of a 3 Page Miller Roll Application

Available in book form, the Guion Miller Roll "Plus" by Bob Blankenship is about $30.00 ; Dawes Roll "Plus" by Bob Blankenship is also about $30.00. Contact your local bookstore or order direct from Cherokee Roots, P.O. Box 525, Cherokee N.C. 28719. Phone (704) 497-9709. The Blankenship family (Eastern band of Cherokees) also offers a research service pertaining to these and other rolls.

Morrison's Indian Research, P.O. Box 41, Boaz, Alabama 35957 Phone 205-593-7336 is another service that offers economical roll and records searches. (Robert and Sue Morrison are members of the Cherokee Tribe of Northeast Alabama).

If you are fortunate enough to find a family member's name listed on either of these rolls, be sure to order copies of the applications completed by the commission to establish their roll entrees. Use the roll name and number shown. These often contain a store of other valuable family information.

The Guion Miller Roll documents are also available in book form as follows: Jordan, Jerry Wright. Cherokee by Blood: Records of Eastern Cherokee Ancestry in the U.S. Court of Claims, 1906-1910 (8 volumes) v.1. Bowie, MD: Heritage Books, 1987-. Contents: v. 1. Applications 1 to 1550 — v. 2. Applications 1551 to 4200 —v. 3. Applications 4201 to 7250 — v. 4. Applications 7251 to 10170 — v. 5. Applications 10171 to 13260 — v. 6. Applications 13261 to 16745 — v. 7. Applications 16746 to 20100 — v. 8. Applications 20101 to 23800. These volumes are available from Heritage Books, 1540 East Pointer Ridge Pl, Suite 400, Bowie, MD 20716 Phone (301) 390-7709. Cost is $34 per volume (paperback).

Churchill Roll, 1908. Prepared by Frank C. Churchill as a listing of Eastern Cherokee to "Certify Members" of the Eastern Band. Two rolls contain accepted and rejected members; both English and Indian names. (Like the Hester roll listed earlier, this census has lots of information).

Federal Census 1910 T-624, 1,784 rolls, Indian Schedules are at the end of the identified Enumeration District ED (Use the Federal Census Index Books for ED of County of Residence.)

Federal Census 1920 T-625, 8,585 rolls, Native American Indians may be identified as Black, Indian, Other, or white.

Baker Roll, 1924. Taken pursuant to an act of June 4, 1924, this was supposed to be the "final Roll" of the Eastern Cherokee. The land was to be allotted and all were to become citizens.Fortunately, the Eastern Cherokee avoided the termination procedures, unlike their brothers and sisters in the Cherokee Nation West. **The Baker Roll Revised serves as the current membership basis of the Eastern Band of Cherokee Indians in North Carolina**.

5-128

CENSUS of the Eastern Cherokee Indians of Cherokee, N.C. Agency,
on June 30 1923, taken by James E. Henderson Superintendent
(Name.) (Official title.)

NUMBER. Last.	NUMBER. Present.	INDIAN NAME	ENGLISH NAME	RELATIONSHIP.	DATE OF BIRTH.	SEX.
1	1		Ahnetonah, Nancy	Wid.	1873	f
2	2		Allen, Will	Hus.	1845	m
3	3		" , Sallie	Wife	1851	f
4	4		Allen , John	Hus.	1871	m
5	5		" , Eva	wife	1884	f
6	6		Allison, Nannie I.	wife	1883	f
7	7		" , Roy Robert	son	1904	m
8	8		" , Albert Monroe	"	1907	m
9	9		" , Ida May	dau.	1909	f
10	10		" , Felix Wilbur	son	1912	m
11	11		" , Boyce Jackson	"	1914	m
12	12		" , Nora Magnalia	dau.	1916	f
940	13	Husband white	Allison, Bessie Matthews	wife	190[illegible]	f
941	14		" , [illegible]	[illegible]	[illegible]	[illegible]

Sample Page from Baker Roll, 1924

The 1900 Federal Census

This particular U.S. census, available on microfilm at many libraries, has been listed separately because it contains a vast amount of information regarding all Indian tribes as well as Cherokee. With the exception of Oklahoma, there is a separate section at the end of each county of each state listing it's Native American residents. In the Oklahoma section, Natives in all areas outside of the territory of the Five Civilized Tribes (Cherokee, Creek, Choctaw, Chickasaw and Seminole) are shown grouped at the end of the microfilm (microfilm number 1241344). Residents of the Five Civilized Tribes are shown at the end of the entire census after the listings for the state of Wyoming... the Cherokees are on microfilm numbers 1241843, 1241844, 1241845, and 1241846. Keep in mind that there may have been many not enrolled and residing in various states. These will be listed at the end of their county within the microfilms for their state of residence, provided they did not hide their native heritage.

The following information is included:

1. Both English and Indian names of all family members in the household.
2. Relationship of each family member to the head-of-household.
3. Age and birth dates by year and month.
4. Number of times married.
5. Length of marriage.
6. Listings for any plural spouses for each spouse in household.
7. Place of birth and parents place of birth.
8. Tribal affiliation and parent's tribe.
9. Degree of white blood, if any.
10. Number of children; number still living.
11. Indication of either fixed or moveable dwelling.
12. Property rented or owned.
13. Employed (by occupation) or "Ration Indian" (indicating federal support).
14. Length of unemployment if unemployed.
15. Ability to read, write or speak English.

Records Other Than Census Rolls

Numerous other records are available in the National Archives which include records of the Bureau of Indian Affairs, U.S. Army Mobile Units, Supreme Court, U.S. District Courts, U.S. Court of Appeals, U.S. Court of Claims, and Veterans Administration. Since the Cherokee Indians were not usually subject to state courts, their civil and criminal court records are normally found in the Federal Court records.

The Bureau of Indian Affairs records include the Indian Removal records, Land Division , Enrollment of the Eastern Cherokee, Law and Probate Division (this deals with the heirs of deceased Indian allottees), Civilization Division, Indian Civil War Claims, Statistics Division, Finance Division, and the Miscellaneous Division. Bureau of Indian Affairs Field Office records available for Cherokees include Cherokee Agency, East located at FARC, Atlanta and Cherokee Agency, West, located at the National Archives in Washington.

In 1938, the Adjutant General's Office transferred its collection of Confederate records to the National Archives. While many of the Confederate records were destroyed before seizure by the Union Army, some records still exist. Roll 74, Compiled Records Showing Service of Military Units in Confederate Organizations contains information about the Indian organizations.Also, compiled military service records have been reproduced on microfilm by the National Archives that include service records of Confederate soldiers, Confederate States Army Casualties, and also documents pertaining to battles in Indian Territory.

(CONFEDERATE.)

L | 1 Cherokee Mtd. Vols. | C. S. A.

Laugh at Mush

Pvt, (2d) Co. B, 1 Reg't Cherokee Mounted Vols.

Appears on

Company Muster Roll

of the organization named above,

for Nov 30 1862 to June 30, 1863

dated June 30 1863

Enlisted:

When July 12, 1862

Where Ft Davis

By whom Capt J. N. Wells

Period 2 years

Last paid:

By whom Maj Vore

To what time ____________, 186 .

Present or absent

Remarks: Absent sick at Canadian since June 25

The 1st Regiment Cherokee Mounted Volunteers (also known as Watie's Regiment; as the 2d Regiment Cherokee Mounted Rifles, Arkansas, and as the 1st Regiment Cherokee Mounted Rifles or Riflemen) was organized July 12, 1861, for twelve months, and reorganized July 12, 1862, for two years. Five companies that were temporarily attached to this regiment after the reorganization are reported to have been assigned, February 3, 1863, to the 2d Regiment Cherokee Mounted Volunteers.

Book mark: ____________

J. N. Wilkinson

Copyist.

(612)

4360

Muster Roll Document from Cherokee Mounted Volunteers, C.S.A.

An excellent text on this subject is "*The Confederate Cherokees - John Drew's Regiment of Mounted Rifles,*" by W. Craig Gaines, Louisiana State University Press (1989).

Military records for individuals who served since 1900 are housed at the Military Personnel Records Center, 9700 Page Boulevard, St. Louis, MO 63132. The American Indian Veterans Association, P.O. Box 543, Isleta, MN 87022, Phone 505-869-9284 can also be a source of information.

Recognize that many persons with some degree of Indian Blood are not mentioned in any federal records because they were not officially recognized as a tribal member or they severed their tribal connections by moving away from the bulk of their tribe. The U. S. Bureau of Indian Affairs classifies these Cherokees as "Category four" Native Americans and states, *"information about Indian ancestry of individuals in Category four is more difficult to locate. This is primarily because the federal government has never maintained a list of all the persons of Cherokee Indian descent, indicating their tribal affiliation, degree of Indian blood or other data."* They go on to say that *"during the removal, a number remained in the southeast and gathered in North Carolina where they purchased land and continued to live. Others went into the Appalachian Mountains to escape being moved west and many of their descendants may still live there now."*

The National Archives records listed herein have been microfilmed for preservation purposes and to facilitate copying. Microfilm beginning with a "M" or "T" number can only be purchased from the National Archives Publication Sales Branch in Washington, DC. For microfilm beginning with "7 RA" contact the National Archives - Fort Worth Texas Branch for purchases. These films can be purchased on per roll cost basis and many can be obtained on a loan basis through your local library. Before visiting a regional archive center, check to be sure they have the records you wish to research.

The Indian Archives in the Oklahoma Historical Society, Oklahoma City (See address in following *Selected Archives Section*), contain about 3 million manuscripts and 6 thousand bound volumes of Indian documents.This is the largest collection of Indian documents in the United States outside of the National Archives, and some private collections also are housed there.These include the works of several noted Indian historians as well as an excellent collection of Oklahoma newspapers. A comprehensive listing of most of this material - *Guide to Cherokee Indian Records Microfilm Collection* (1996) by Sharron Standifer Ashton - is available from Ashton Books, 3812 Northwest Sterling, Norman, OK. 73072-1240.

Tennessee State Library and Archives in Nashville (See *Selected Archives Address Listings*) offers an excellent selection of material for Cherokee research. In addition to many of the National Archives Source microfilms listed earlier, the following references are available there:

Records of the Cherokee Agency in Tennessee, 1801-1835. NA # M208, TSLA Mf. # 52, reel 13.

Hoskins, Shirley. "Reservations." Gwy Ye: Cherokee Blood Newsletter 14 (1987): 13-23, E99.C5 C99.

TSLA Microfilm # 815 (Cherokee Collection), Reel One includes:

Surveys (Incomplete)
Spoilation Claims.
List of Persons Who Have Not Received Any Compensation for Improvements Removed, 1824.

TSLA Microfilm # 815 (Cherokee Collection), Reel Eight contains genealogy information on the following surnames: Ridge, Ross, Sequoyah (George Guess), Lovely, Meigs, Clingan, Hildebrand, Lowery, McLemore, McNair, Parks, Taylor, Vann, and Walker).

Hoskins, Shirley Coats. Cherokee Property Evaluations,1836 Chattanooga, Tennessee, 1984. E99.C5 C54.

McGhee, Lucy Kate. Cherokee and Creek Indians. Returns of Property Left in Tennessee and Georgia, 1838.E93.M32.

Martini, Don. Southeastern Indian Notebook: A Biographical and Genealogical Guide to the Five Civilized Tribes, 1685-1865. Ripley, MS: Ripley Printing Company, 1986. E78.565 M376 1986.

Cherokee National Capital, Tahlequah, OK built in 1867.
(Photo by author).

Addresses for Selected Archives:

National Archives
7th and Pennsylvania Ave.
Washington, DC. 20408
Telephone 205-501-5402

National Archives—Alaska Region
654 West Third Avenue
Anchorage, AK 99501
Telephone: 907-271-2441

National Archives—Central Plains Region
2312 East Bannister Road
Kansas City, MO 64131
Telephone: 816-926-6272

National Archives—Great Lakes Region
7358 South Pulaski Road
Chicago, IL 60629
Telephone: 312-581-7816

National Archives—Mid Atlantic Region
9th and Market Streets, Room 1350
Philadelphia, PA 19107
Telephone: 215-597-3000

National Archives—New England Region
380 Trapelo Road
Waltham, MA 02154
Telephone: 617-647-8100

National Archives—Northeast Region
201 Varick Street
New York, NY 10014
Telephone: 212-337-1300

National Archives—Pacific Northwest Reg.
6125 Sand Point Way, NE
Seattle, WA 98115
Telephone: 206-526-6507

National Archives—Pacific Sierra Region
1000 Commodore Drive
San Bruno, CA 94066
Telephone: 415-876-9009

National Archives—Pacific Southwest Reg.
24000 Avila Road
Laguna Niquel, CA 92656
Telephone: 714-643-4241

National Archives—Rocky Mountain Region
Building 48-Denver Federal Center
Denver, CO 80255-0307
Telephone: 303-236-0817

National Archives—Southeast Region
1557 St. Joseph Avenue
East Point, GA 30344
Telephone: 404-763-7477

National Archives—Southwest Region
501 West Felix Street
Fort Worth, TX 76115
Telephone: 817-334-5525

Alabama (Mobile Public Library)
History and Genealogy Division
701 Government Street
Mobile, AL 36602
Telephone: 205-434-7093

Arkansas State University Museum Library and Archives
P.O. Box 490
State University
Jonesboro, AR 72467
Telephone 501-972-2074

Georgia State Archives
330 Capitol Avenue, S.E.
Atlanta, GA 30334
Telephone 404-656-2358

New Echota Historic Site Library
1211 Chatsworth Hwy
Calhoun, Ga. 30701
Telephone 404-629-8151

Kentucky Historical Society Library
300 Broadway
Frankfort, KY 40602
Telephone 502-564-3016

Mississippi Dept of Archives and History
P.O.Box 571
Jackson, MS 39205-0571
Telephone 601-359-6876

Museum of the Cherokee Indian Library
P.O. Box 770-A
U.S.Hwy 441 North
Cherokee, NC 28719
Telephone 704-497-3481

Native American Resource Center Library
Pembroke State University
College Road
Pembroke, NC 28372
Telephone 919-521-4214

North Carolina State Library
Genealogy & Archives Branch
109 East Jones St.
Raleigh, NC 27601-2807
Telephone 919-733-7222

Schiele Museum Reference Library
Center for Southeastern Studies
P.O. Box 953
1500 East Garrison Blvd.
Gastonia, NC 28053-0953
Telephone 704-866-6900

Oklahoma Historical Society
2100 N. Lincoln Blvd.
Oklahoma City, OK 73105
Telephone 405-521-2491

Thomas Gilcrease Institute
American History and Art
1400 Gilcrease Museum Rd.
Tulsa, OK 74127
Telephone 918-582-3122

Cherokee National Historical Society
P.O. Box 515
Tahlequah, OK 74465
Telephone: 918-456-6007

South Carolina Dept of Archives and History
P.O.Box 11669
1430 Senate St.
Columbia, SC 29211-1669
Telephone 803-734-8596

Tennessee State Archives and Library
403 7th Avenue North
Nashville, TN 37219
Telephone 615- 741-2764

Red Clay State Historical Park Library
Route 6, Box 733
Cleveland, TN 37311
Telephone 615-472-2626

Amon Carter Museum Photographic Archives
3501 Camp Bowie Boulevard
Ft. Worth, TX 76107-2631
Telephone: 817-738-1933

Virginia State Library & Archives
11th Street at Capitol Square
Richmond, VA 23219-3491
Telephone 804-786-2306

Most archives have lists of private researchers available for hire upon request. National archives personnel are particularly careful about recommending specific researchers for hire, but the use of a little diplomacy can go a long way toward acquiring this information.

To Find Other Groups Among the Cherokee:

Prevost, Toni Jollay. The Delaware & Shawnee Admitted to Cherokee Citizenship and the Related Wyandotte & Moravian Delaware. Bowie, MD (1540-E Pointer Ridge Place, 20716): Heritage Books, 1993. ISBN 1556137613. [130] p. Not indexed.

Stevenson, Noel C. Genealogical Evidence: A Guide to the Standard of Proof Relating to Pedigrees, Ancestry, Heirship, and Family History. Rev. ed. Laguna Hills, CA (P.O. Box 2837, 92654): Aegean Park Press, 1989. ISBN 089412160X; 0894121596 (pbk.). [239] p. Indexed.

Walton-Raji, Angela Y. Black Indian Genealogy Research : African American Ancestors Among the Five Civilized Tribes. Bowie, MD (1540-E Pointer Ridge Place, 20716): Heritage Books, Inc., 1993. ISBN 1556138563.

Eakle, Arlene; and Cerny, Johni. The Source: A Guidebook of American Genealogy. Salt Lake City, UT: Ancestry Publishing Co., 1984. LC 84-70206; ISBN 0916489000. 786 p. Indexed.

Recommended Texts for Researching Cherokee Indian Ancestry

The recommended texts listed herein include some Indian history references for some of the states because they often mention Cherokees by name. If you plan to borrow materials through inter-library Loan, advise your librarian that some of these may be special collections materials available only at the University of Oklahoma Libraries and University of Tulsa Libraries.

If you wish to purchase any of these books, sources include:

Cherokee Braves Trading Post, P. O. Box 309, Weber Falls, Oklahoma 74470, Phone 918-464-2025.

Cherokee Publications, P.O. Box 430-N, Cherokee, NC 28719, Phone 704-488-8856.

The Cherokee Nation Gift Shop, Tahlequah, Oklahoma, Phone 918- 456-2793.

Cherokee Heritage Center, P.O. Box 515, Tahlequah, OK 74465-0515, Phone 918- 456-6007.

Museum of the Cherokee Indian, Cherokee, N.C. Phone 704-497-3481.

General Guides and Bibliography

Cherokee Roots / Bob Blankenship. 2nd ed. (Cherokee, NC : Author, 1992, 2 v.). Contents: v. 1. Eastern Cherokee rolls (includes 1817 Reservation Rolls, 1817-1835 Emigration Roll, 1835 Henderson Roll, 1848 Mullay Roll, 1851 Siler Roll, 1852 Chapman Roll, 1869 Swetland Roll, 1883 Hester Roll, 1908 Churchill Roll, 1909 Guion Miller East, 1924 Baker Roll, Enrollment procedures of Eastern Band — v. 2. 1851 Old Settler Roll, 1852 Drennen Roll by family name, 1898-1914 combination Dawes and Guion Miller Rolls, Enrollment procedures of the Cherokee Nation.

Records of the Cherokee Indian Agency in Tennessee 1801-1835/Marybelle W. Chase (Tulsa, OK). Lists and Registers transcribed from National Archives BIA records).

The Cherokees: A Critical Bibliography. / Raymond D. Fogelson. (Bloomington, Published for the Newberry Library by Indiana University Press, 1978. Series: Bibliographical series (Newberry Library. Center for the History of the American Indian).

The Five Civilized Tribes: a bibliography / Mary Huffman. (Oklahoma City, OK: Library Resources Division, Oklahoma Historical Society, 1991).

Guide to the Historical Records of Oklahoma / Bradford Koplowitz.(Bowie, M: Heritage Books, 1990).

Oklahoma history: a bibliography / Mary Huffman, Brian Basore.(Oklahoma City, OK: Library Resources Division, Oklahoma Historical Society, 1991).

Our Native Americans and Their Records of Genealogical Value / E. Kay Kirkham. (Logan, Utah: Everton Publishers,

1980-1984.LC 81-128028; 2 v.). Contents: v. 1. Federal Government records, Oklahoma Historical Society records, Genealogical Society of Utah listings — v. 2. [without special title] [Using this book with the National Archives catalog on American Indians, will provide citations for most major sources of records.

Recommended Genealogy Texts

Cherokee Planters in Georgia 1832-1838 Vol. 2/ Don L. Shadburn/. (Cumming, GA: Author, rev. 1996, LC 89-51794)[Note: Available from author: P.O. Box 3121. Cumming, GA 30128]

Genealogy of "Old & New Cherokee Indian Families" / by George Morrison Bell, Sr. 1st ed. (Bartlesville, OK : Author, 1972, LC 78-189676).

History of the Cherokee Indians and Their Legends and Folk Lore /Emmett Starr. (Oklahoma City, OK : The Warden Co, 1921; reprinted by: New York : Kraus, 1969).

Indian Blood Volumes I and II / by Richard Pangburn (Louisville, Ky: Butler Books 1996) ISBN 1-884532-05-5. These can be ordered directly from the author: 404 Greer Rd., Bardstown, Ky 40004.

Old Cherokee Families : "Old Families and Their Genealogy" : reprinted from History of the Cherokee Indians and their legends and folk lore / Emmet Starr ; with a comprehensive index compiled by J.J. Hill. (Norman, OK : University of Oklahoma Foundation, 1968. Emmet Starr's original edition was published in 1921).

Cherokee Connections: An Introduction to Genealogical Sources pertaining to Cherokee Ancestors/Myra Vanderpool Gormerly. (Tacoma, WA (207 S. 119th St., 98444): Family Historian Books, 1995. ISBN 1886952553. Phone 800-535-0118.

Censuses, Rolls, Claims, Newspapers, Journals, and Indexes

1842 Cherokee claims: Saline District / Marybelle W. Chase. (Tulsa, OK: Author, 1988). [Note-see next listing].

1842 Cherokee claims: Tahlequah District / Marybelle W. Chase. (Tulsa,OK: Author 1989). [Researchers should note that the author has compiled booklets for several other districts. These were handwritten reports of claims filed by individuals for loss of property not included in valuations before the removal. Most will show residence in the east before removal. Transcribed from originals in The Tennessee State Library, Nashville, TN].

1880 and 1890 census, Canadian District, Cherokee Nation, Indian Territory. / transcribed by Sharon Standifer Ashton. (Oklahoma City, OK: Oklahoma Genealogical Society, 1978. Series: Special publication (Oklahoma Genealogical Society), no. 5).

Cherokee Advocate [microform]. Vol. 1, no. 1 (Sept. 26, 1844) - (March 3, 1906). Tahlequah, Cherokee Nation, s.n. Weekly. In English and Cherokee (in Cherokee syllabary). Issued with: Cherokee messenger (Aug. 1844 - May 1846); Cherokee almanac (1840, 1847, 1855, 1860); Choctaw Baptist hymn book; Choctaw intelligencer (Oct. 15, 1851). Contents: Reel 1. May 1, 1845 - June 27, 1877 — Reel 2. July 4, 1877-June 29, 1883 — Reel 3. July 6, 1883 - Dec. 21, 1901 — Reel 4. Jan. 4, 1902 - March 3, 1906. Suspended publication Sept. 28, 1853-April 22, 1870; Jan. 1875 - March 4, 1876. Microform. Oklahoma City, Oklahoma State Historical Society. 4 microfilm reels; 35 mm).

Cherokee Emigration Rolls, 1817-1835. / transcribed by Jack D.Baker. (Oklahoma City, OK : Baker Pub. Co., 1977).

Cherokee Nation 1890 census: index of persons living under permit in the Cooweescoowee and Delaware Districts / Rosalie Wagner.(Vinita, OK: Northeastern Oklahoma Genealogical Society, 1986).

Cherokee Nation Births and Deaths, 1884-1901: abstracted from Indian Chieftain and Daily Chieftain newspapers / by Dixie Bogle (Vinita, OK: Northeast Oklahoma Genealogical Society, 1980).

Cherokee Nation Marriages, 1884-1901: abstracted from Indian Chieftain and Daily Chieftain newspapers / by Dixie Bogle and Dorothy Nix. (Vinita, OK : Abraham Coryell Chapter NSDAR, [1980]).

Our People and Where They Rest / James and Maxine Tyner and Alice Timmons/12 Volumes (vol 1-8, Norman, OK: American Indian Institute; vol 9-12, Muskogee, OK: Chigau Press), 1968-1985. [Note: These are guides to cemeteries in Indian Territories of N.E. Oklahoma showing locations of graves by name, birth and death dates].

Cherokee Reservees / David Keith Hampton. (Oklahoma City, OK: Baker Pub. Co., 1979); copy at McFarlin Library, University of Tulsa. (E99.C5H23 1979).

Final Rolls of Citizens and Freedmen of the Five Civilized Tribes in Indian Territory [microform], (as approved by the Secretary of the Interior on or before March 4, 1907, with supplements dated September 25, 1914) / United States. Commission to the Five Civilized Tribes. (Washington, DC: National Archives, 1961. 3 reels. 35 mm. Series: National Archives microfilm publications, T529). Contents: Reel 1. Choctaw and Chickasaw rolls — Reel 2. Cherokee rolls — Reel 3. Creek and Seminole rolls. [Dawes Commission rolls].

Genealogical Data extracted from "Muskogee Weekly Phoenix" Indian Territory / compiled by Sheri Siebold. (Muskogee, OK: Muskogee County Genealogical Society, 1985). Contents: v.1. 1888-1892.

Index to Marriages, First United States Court Northern District, Muskogee, Indian Territory, 1890-1907. (Oklahoma City, OK Oklahoma Genealogical Society, 1980, Series: Special publication (Oklahoma Genealogical Society) no. 6; LC 83-150507). v. 1. Marriage Books A, B, B-1, C (5 Jul 1890 - 19 Sep 1894) with abstracts of some marriages and divorces from inventory of Creek and Cherokee National Records, 1869-1894.

Index to Payment Roll for Old Settler Cherokee, 1896 / transcribed by Marybelle W. Chase. (Tulsa, OK: Author, 1989).

Cherokee Old Settler Annuity Roll 1851 /transcribed by Marybelle W. Chase from National Archives records regarding 1896 payment of Old Settlers. (Tulsa, OK: Author, 1989).

Index to The Cherokee Advocate. (Little Rock, AR : American Native Press Archives, University of Arkansas at Little Rock, 1987); books in files (2nd-3rd ser.). Contents: 2nd series (1870-1875) — 3rd series v. 1-3 (1 Mar 1876 - 26 Mar 1879).

The Intruders: The Illegal Residents of the Cherokee Nation, 1866-1907 / Nancy Hope Sober. (Ponca City, OK: Cherokee Books, 1991. LC 90-84850).

Journal of Cherokee Studies. Vol. 1 (summer 1976)-. [Cherokee, N.C.], Museum of the Cherokee Indian. Quarterly).

Oklahoma Genealogical Society Quarterly. v.6, no.1 (Mar 1961)- (Oklahoma City, OK: Oklahoma Historical Society).

Southeastern Native American Exchange (S.E.N.A.) - (Mobile, AL: Jacqueline Hines, publisher. Quarterly. Address: P.O.Box 16124, Mobile, AL 36616-2424).

The Cherokee Tracer. v. 1, no. 1 (Winter 1991)- (Tulsa, OK :Marybelle W. Chase, editor and publisher, 1991- Quarterly. Address: 5802 E. 22nd Pl, Tulsa,OK 74114)

The Chronicles of Oklahoma. 1 (Jan 1921)- (Oklahoma City, OK: Oklahoma Historical Society, Quarterly.)

Tulsa annuals. v. 1 (Sep 1966)- (Tulsa, OK : Tulsa Genealogical Society. Three times a year).

[Note: The above six periodicals provide an on-going supply of valuable information for researchers. I highly recommend that you subscribe to them if at all possible)!

Probate records... Northern District Cherokee Nation / Orpha Jewell Wever; indexed by Rosalie Wagner. (Vinita, OK: Northeast Oklahoma Genealogical Society, 1982-<1983>). Contents: v. 1. 1892-1904 — v. 2. 1904-1908.

Those Who Cried, the 16,000, a record of the individual Cherokees listed in the United States official census of the Cherokee Nation conducted in 1835 / James W. Tyner. ([Norman, OK]: Chi-ga-u Inc., 1974).

History

[Note: These texts often contain family surnames not found on any official rolls]:

Advancing the Frontier, 1830-1860 / Grant Foreman. (Norman, OK: University of Oklahoma Press, 1933).

America's Exiles: Indian colonization in Oklahoma / Arrell Morgan Gibson. (Oklahoma City, OK: Oklahoma Historical Society, 1976. Series: The Oklahoma series, vol. III. LC 76-11417).

And Still the Waters Run / Angie Debo. (Princeton, NJ: Princeton University Press, 1940; reprint in 1984: Norman, OK: University of Oklahoma Press).

A History of the Indians of the United States / Angie Debo. [1st ed.]. (Norman, OK: University of Oklahoma Press, 1970. Series: Civilization of the American Indian series, v. 106. LC 73-108802).

A Political History of the Cherokee Nation, 1838-1907 / Morris L. Wardell. 1st ed. (Norman, OK: University of Oklahoma Press, 1938. Series: Civilization of the American Indian series, v. 17).

Cherokee Cavaliers, forty years of Cherokee history as told in the correspondence of the Ridge-Watie-Boudinot family / Edward Everett Dale & Gaston Litton. 1st ed. (Norman, OK: University of Oklahoma Press, 1939). Series: Civilization of the American Indian series, v. 19).

Cherokee Nation of Indians / Charles C. Royce. (Chicago, IL Aldine Pub. Co., 1975. Series: Native American Library; A Smithsonian Institution Press Book. LC75-20708).

Cherokee Indian Removal from the Lower Hiwassee Valley/ Robert C. White.(Cleveland, TN, 1973).

Cherokees of the Old South: A People in Transition/ Henry Thompson Malone. (Athens, GA: University of Georgia Press, 1956).

Cherokee Removal, Before and After / William L. Anderson (Athens, GA: University of Georgia Press, 1991).

Cherokee Tragedy: The Ridge Family and the Decimation of a People / Thurman Wilkins. 2nd ed., rev. (Norman, OK: University of Oklahoma Press, 1986. Series: Civilization of the American Indian series, v. 169. LC 85-20260).

Cherokees: An Illustrated History / Billy M. Jones and Odie B. Faulk. (Muskogee, OK: The Five Civilized Tribes Museum, 1984).

Cherokee Footprints, Volume I, The Principal People "Ani-Yunwiya." /Charles O. Walker. The author.

Cherokee Footprints, Volume II, Home and Hearth/ Charles O. Walker. The author.

Chief Bowles and the Texas Cherokees / Mary Whatley Clarke. 1st ed. (Norman, OK: University of Oklahoma Press, 1971. Series: Civilization of the American Indian series, v. 113).

Dawn of the Tennessee Valley and Tennessee History /Samuel C. Williams. (Johnson City, TN: Watauga Press, 1937).

Hard times in Oklahoma: The Depression Years / Kenneth E. Hendrickson, Jr. (Oklahoma City, OK: Oklahoma Historical Society, 1983. Series: The Oklahoma Series. LC 83-060262).

History of Hamilton County and Chattanooga/ Zella Armstrong. (Chattanooga: Lookout Mountain Publishing, 1931-40).

Indian Removal: The Emigration of the Five Civilized Tribes of Indians / Grant Foreman. (Norman, OK: University of Oklahoma Press, 1932. Series: Civilization of the American Indian Series, v.2).

Myths of the Cherokee and Sacred Formulas of the Cherokees / James Mooney. (Nashville, TN: Charles Elder, Bookseller, 1972. Reprint of 19th and 7th annual reports of Bureau of American Ethnology).

New Echota Letters / Jack Frederick Kilpatrick and Anna Gritts Kilpatrick. (Dallas, TX: Southern Methodist University Press, 1968. Selections from the newspaper Cherokee phoenix, 1828-33, including contributions of S. A. Worcester and the newspaper's editor, E. Boudinot).

Oklahoma Place Names / George H. Shirk. (Norman: University of Oklahoma Press, 1981).

Old Frontiers, The Story of the Cherokee Indians from Earliest Times to the Date of Their Removal to the West, 1838 / John P. Brown. (Kingsport, TN: Southern Publishers, 1938).

Passports of Southeastern Pioneers 1770-1823 / Dorothy Williams Potter. (Baltimore, Maryland: Gateway Press, 1982).

Red over Black, Black Slavery Among the Cherokee Indians / R. Halliburton, Jr. (Westport, CT: Greenwood Press, 1977. Series: Contributions in Afro-American and African studies, no. 27).

Red Clay and Rattlesnake Springs: A History of the Cherokee Indians of Bradley County, Tennessee / James F. Corn. (Cleveland, TN: Walsworth Publishing Co, reprinted 1984).

Tennessee's Indian Peoples: From White Contact to Indian Removal, 1540-1840/Ronald N. Satz. (Knoxville, TN, 1979).

The Cherokees / Grace Steele Woodward. [1st ed.]. (Norman, OK: University of Oklahoma Press, [1963], Series: Civilization of the American Indian series, v. 65. LC 63-8986).

The Five Civilized Tribes: Cherokee, Chickasaw, Choctaw, Creek, Seminole / Grant Foreman. 1st ed. (Norman, OK: University of Oklahoma Press, 1934. Series: Civilization of the American Indian series, v. 8).

The Eastern Band of Cherokees, 1819-1900. / John R. Finger. (Knoxville, TN: University of Tennessee Press, 1984. LC 83-10284).

The Cherokee Crown of Tannassy. / William O. Steele. (Winston- Salem, N.C.: J. F. Blair Publisher, 1977).

The Cherokee Indians and Those Who Came After: Notes for a History of Cherokee County, North Carolina, 1835-1860 Nathaniel C. Browder. [New ed.]. (Hayesville, NC: Browder, 1973 i.e. 1974. LC 74-25553).

The Papers of Chief John Ross / edited and with an introduction by Gary E. Moulton. (Norman, OK : University of Oklahoma Press, 1985. 2 v.). Contents: v. 1. 1807-1839 — v. 2. 1840-1866.

The Cherokee People / Thomas E. Mails (New York, N.Y: Marlowe And Co. 1996 edition; ISBN 1-56924-762-5).

The Removal of the Cherokee Indians from Georgia, 1827-1841 / Wilson Lumpkin. (New York, A. M. Kelley, 1971. 2 v. in 1. Reprint of the 1907 ed.).

The Texas Cherokees, A People Between Two Fires, 1819-1840 / Dianna Everett. 1st ed. (Norman, OK: University of Oklahoma Press, 1990. Series: The Civilization of the American Indian series, v. 203).

Trail of Tears, the Rise and Fall of the Cherokee Nation. / John Ehle. 1st ed. (New York: Doubleday, 1988).

"The Wahnenauhi Manuscript: Historical Sketches of the Cherokees, together with some of their Customs, Traditions, and Superstitions" / [Wah-ne-nau-hi (Mrs. Lucy Lowrey Hoyt Keys)]; edited by Jack Frederick Kilpatrick. Smithsonian Institution. Bureau of American Ethnology. Bulletin 196, Anthropological papers, no. 77).

The Cherokee Indian Nation: A Troubled History / Duane H. King. (Knoxville: University of Tennessee Press, 1981, 2nd Printing).

The American Indian in North Carolina / Douglas L. Rights. (Durham: Duke University Press, 1947).

Internet Sources

The rapid advances of electronic information and the advantages it has to offer on the Internet caused much soul searching as to whether to include it in this guide. After careful consideration, I elected to omit it, simply because it is changing so rapidly that any information included herein would no doubt be obsolete by the time of publication. Suffice it to say that a multitude of genealogical data can be had via this source and if you have a home computer, it is worth taking a look at. Simply use any Internet provider, refer to any search vehicle, and type in the word "Cherokee." You will receive listings of everything from the latest advances in popular Jeeps that carry a vehicle model called Cherokee to complete histories of the Cherokee people.

Many of the websites that I have surveyed contain excellent information about our subject and some are a waste of time. Approach them with that in mind and you can quickly determine which ones fit your needs.

Pre-Colonial and Colonial Era Intermarriages

by Brent Cox (Yanusdi), M.A.

As you have already seen, there are several approaches to tracing Cherokee ancestry. This section focuses primarily on precolonial/colonial era intermarriages between Cherokees and British or French. Most references only offer information on Cherokees of the 19th and 20th centuries. While this is important, the majority of us descend from intermarriages that occurred in the 18th century. Thus, many of these kinships came from British or French traders intermarrying with Cherokees.

Through 1776, South Carolina controlled the Cherokee trade, and most of our mixed ancestors were connected to this region. Virginia also supplied a few traders to the Cherokees, and Georgia and North Carolina still fewer. Thus, to locate your ancestors, whether from Georgia, North Carolina, South Carolina, or Virginia, most records of note are related to the South Carolina Indian trade. To begin your search for this era before "rolls" existed, I recommend that you do a surname survey in:

William L. McDowell, Jr. ed. The Colonial Records of South Carolina: Documents relating to Indian Affairs.2 Vols. Columbia: South Carolina Department of Archives and History, 1992. This set, including one other volume, can be purchased from: South Carolina Dept. of Archives & History, P.O. Box 11669, 1430 Senate St., Columbia, S.C. 29211, Phone: 803-734-8590.

If you intend to do a thorough study of your ancestors who may have intermarried with the Cherokees, this 3 volume set is indispensable. It is the most thorough record of British/Cherokee trade available.

Now, here are some other important tips to keep in mind:

1. Always be aware that spellings of names are not always the same in historical records.

   a. English/French surnames vary according to region. EX: Bryant, Briant, Brian, de Bruyant.

   b. All Cherokee names are phonetic spellings of either French or British pronunciation. EX: Chota (the Cherokee capitol), French=Sautee, English=Chota, Cherokee= It-sati (Eet-saw-tee). Personal names also vary according to dialect or region.

   c. The Cherokees had three dialects, and names vary accordingly. EX: YellowBird (a common name), Lower dialect=Cheesquatarone, Upper dialect=Cheesquatalone.

2. Do not assume the origin of your Cherokee blood, nor the degree of blood contained. Family tradition tells us that all our grandmothers were full blood Cherokees, yet by 1900, there were very few full blood Cherokees in existence.

   a. The surname you started with may lead you to another surname. More than likely, your search will end with a significant trader.

   b. Do not assume anything, but be prepared to find conflicting information.

3. Search the regions around the Cherokee nation, and be aware of the fluctuating borders of both the Cherokees and the frontier.

   a. There were four settlement groups in the Cherokee Nation.
   OVERHILLS- East Tennessee on the Little Tennessee River.
   VALLEY- Lower east Tennessee, southwestern North Carolina, and north Georgia.
   LOWER- western South Carolina, and northeastern Georgia.
   MIDDLE- western North Carolina.

   b. All regions around these areas are possible locations to find your ancestor. The Cherokee people were mobile, and moved from place to place within/without the Cherokee Nation.

c. Check all colonial, state and local histories, frontier histories, Indian trade records. Here are some suggestions:

Colonial Records to Search:

Allan D. Chandler, ed. THE COLONIAL RECORDS OF THE STATE OF GEORGIA, Atlanta: Charles P. Boyd Printer, 1914.

Walter Clark, ed. THE STATE RECORDS OF NORTH CAROLINA, New York: AMS Press, 1968.

Kenneth G. Davies, ed. DOCUMENTS OF THE AMERICAN REVOLUTION, 1770-1783, Dublin: Irish University Press, 1976.

Wilmer L. Hall, ed. EXECUTIVE JOURNALS OF THE COUNCIL OF COLONIAL VIRGINIA, Richmond: Commonwealth of Virginia, 1945.

William P. Palmer, ed. VIRGINIA STATE PAPERS AND OTHER MANUSCRIPTS, 1652- 1781, New York: Kraus Reprint Co. 1968.

William L. Saunders, ed. THE COLONIAL RECORDS OF NORTH CAROLINA, New York: AMS Press, 1968.

David Ramsey, THE HISTORY OF SOUTH CAROLINA, Charleston: David Longworth, 1809.

For Western North Carolina

John Preston Arthur, A HISTORY
OF WATAUGA COUNTY, NORTH CAROLINA,
Johnson City: The Overmountain Press, 1992.

For Southwestern Virginia

Lewis Preston Summers, HISTORY OF WASHINGTON COUNTY, VIRGINIA, Johnson City: The Overmountain Press, 1989.

For North Georgia

Don L. Shadburn, UNHALLOWED INTRUSION: A HISTORY OF CHEROKEE FAMILIES IN FORSYTH COUNTY, GA. Cumming, GA.: Don Shadburn, P.O. Box 762, Cumming, Ga. 30130.

For Tennessee

There are several suggestions for this region that also give information on the frontiers and much of early Tennessee:

John Haywood, THE CIVIL AND POLITICAL HISTORY OF TENNESSEE, Knoxville: The Tenase Company, 1969.

J.G.M. Ramsey, THE ANNALS OF TENNESSEE, Knoxville: East Tennessee Historical Society, 1967.

Albigence Waldo Putnam, THE HISTORY OF MIDDLE TENNESSEE: OR LIFE AND TIMES OF GENERAL JAMES ROBERTSON, New York: Arno Press, 1971.

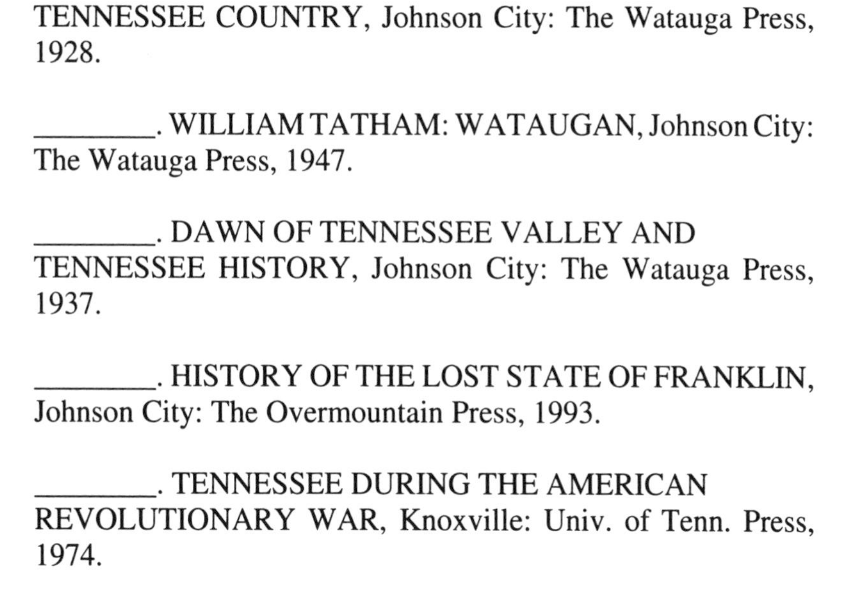

Samuel Cole Williams, EARLY TRAVELS IN THE TENNESSEE COUNTRY, Johnson City: The Watauga Press, 1928.

________. WILLIAM TATHAM: WATAUGAN, Johnson City: The Watauga Press, 1947.

________. DAWN OF TENNESSEE VALLEY AND TENNESSEE HISTORY, Johnson City: The Watauga Press, 1937.

________. HISTORY OF THE LOST STATE OF FRANKLIN, Johnson City: The Overmountain Press, 1993.

________. TENNESSEE DURING THE AMERICAN REVOLUTIONARY WAR, Knoxville: Univ. of Tenn. Press, 1974.

4. Do not restrict your search, but record anything you find on your surname. Your ancestor may be using both an Indian name and an English/French name. Indian names are often evocative of nature or personality traits.

5. The Cherokee clans were based on a matrilineal system (traced thru the mother's line).
  a. In the 1750s, this system began to change due to intermarriage with European Americans.
  b. While Cherokees kept traditional matrilineal oral records, mixed Cherokees often used both patrilineal and matrilineal notations.
  c. Many Cherokee traders also had two families: a Cherokee family, and another located in South Carolina or Virginia.

6. Do not stop searching because your ancestor disappears off the records - there were no written records within the Cherokee Nation during this period.
  a. You must rely on European-American records to locate your ancestor.

b. Do not always accept everything at face value, and be totally objective.

c. When your ancestor (surnames) can not be found on traditional records, this is usually a good sign that they may be found within the Cherokee Nation.

d. Remember that most Upper Creek traders had Cherokee wives.

7. When you ask your older relatives and those connected to the suspected line where they think your Cherokee ancestry came from, recognize that anything they tell you may help, even if it appears as simple trivia. Remember that you were the one chosen to carry this lineage forward and it is your duty to do so. Make genealogical connections and queries to get help from others. Try to enlist the help of all your relatives with the same surname.

8. Understand Cherokee traditions and attempt to recognize traits that exist in your current family. Your ancestors want to be remembered, so let them assist you in your work. Be aware of dreams and visions that might guide you. This may sound ridiculous, but believe me, within the Cherokee culture, it is a fact that is well known and respected. Even animals may offer clues to lead you to your kin.

Let your heart lead you as well. Native American people traditionally have "feelings" that lead us to where we want to go. Others often do not understand this phenomenon, but it is true, nonetheless. Above all, be aware that you must depend on more than traditional genealogical methods to reach the destination you seek. Cherokee genealogy, as well as all Native genealogy, is not traditional.

9. Search all abstracts, journals, and memoirs available on Cherokee families. Read the JOURNAL OF CHEROKEE STUDIES, 16 volumes available at some libraries or for sale by CHEROKEE PUBLICATIONS, Cherokee, North Carolina. This series contains many genealogical abstracts and articles about prominent Cherokees that you will not see elsewhere. Because it

was advantageous for early traders to marry prominent Cherokees, most did so, so be aware that you could be kin to any of the prominent chieftains (head men). Also, be aware that one Cherokee may possess many titles or names i.e., Ostenaco can be found as Mankiller, Ootacite, Tacite, or Outacite. All four of these terms are the same word.

10. Every text that you search includes a bibliography. Make sure to search the bibliographies for other sources that might help you. Granted, this can be very time consuming, but I urge you to search every available text.

AFFIDAVIT OF WILLIAM THOMSON

|52| Council Chamber

Wm. Thomson being duely sworn, declareth that for some Time past he had been at Tomasse, a Town in the Cherokee Nation, not as a Trader, but Servant to William McDowell.

That on Wednesday or Thursday after Mr. Maxwell went from Tomasse, to go over the Mountains, he heard at Kewee that the Indians designed to kill all the white People, which Information he had of Wm. Mr. Smith. That the Reason given by the Cherokees for their Resolution of killing the white Men was because they said this Government supplied the Creeks with Ammunition, and withheld it from them.

That one Edwd. Broadway was the first that brot the Deponent an Account of four white Men being killed by the Indians, that one Chiottohee was the Man that killed Murphey, that the Indian Messenger when he returned over the Mountains, would not stop anywhere, till he came to Kewee. That Moses Kellingham advised the Deponent to save his Life by immediately makeing his Escape. That thereupon the Deponent set off from Tomassee about Midnight. That he did all he could to persuade John Bryant to go with him, but he said if they took a way his Goods, they must also take his Life, therefore that he would remain in the Nation and see the Upshot. That however Moses Kellingham did set off with the Deponent. When Smith was ask't the Reason for the Indians taking the Resolution of killing the white People, he said these Indians were so much indebted to the white People for Goods, that they imagined if they killed them the Debt was paid. The four white People who was killed, were murdered in one Day in their several Towns viz.; Murphey in Conohoy, Bartholw. Hughs in Stecoew, Thomas Langley in Kittna, and Charles Grores in Kittna.

That before the Deponent left the Nation, Beamer left his own Town and came past Toxoway. That James Thomson came to Tomasse to acquaint the Traders that Beamer was gone off, and named all the white People and Traders to follow him. That as Bryan†told the Deponent, James Maxwell came to Oycree, in order to go off, that some had or said they were informed by some of the Indians, that the Talks of the Indians against the white People were very bad. That Beamer set off 3 Nights after Maxwell, that on the Day Beamer |53| fled, and the Deponent did the same, that after the Deponent

Old Colonial Records like this excerpt from the South Carolina Indian Affairs Documents (1750-52) can offer clues to your ancestor's occupation, movements and location.

The Masters Palette

by Kate Brantley Alcock (Ayasta)

Creation was the artwork from the hand of the master as he covered the land.
Taking the colours of the universe faster than the eye could blink.
The dark blanket of the spaces glimmer in sync with the masters dream.
He painted the colours of the peoples to be tan, brown and cream.
He wanted all of this children to lean on his hand.
The children covered the land creating a multicolored blanket.
He saw the Cherokee children as a tiny trinket
as a grain of sand
part of the plan of the soul of the universe.
The Cherokee children looked up as His hand painted the sky
and knew why they could rely on Him.
This is the pride of the Cherokee . . .
They are the seed of the tree
that will spread and be prepared to see
His hand again cover the land.

Read, Read, Read and Follow the Clues!

Finding your ancestor's name on a federal roll can be elating, but don't stop there. Be sure to check for other documents that may be available in the National Archives and elsewhere. For some people, there is a multitude of documents to be found, for others, nothing.

The importance of reading everything you can get your hands on regarding Cherokee history cannot be over emphasized. This research can take you many places and more deeply into your own unique origins. Equally important, when you are least expecting it, a new clue can leap from the pages, begging for further investigation. I've had this happen many times and often the payoff was very rewarding.

Written records on my Cherokee Grandmother Lucy Bryant are very meager, but that is not necessarily true with everyone's ancestors. To illustrate just a few examples of what you can find and the importance of letting one clue lead you to another, let's use one of the other reservee's names on the same 1817 Reservation Roll that my grandmother's name appears on. Three names below Lucy Bryant's you will notice the name "*Bryant Ward.*"

The roll itself establishes that in 1817, this individual lived on a 640-acre reserve in Georgia designated as "Chatahouchee." To attempt to find out more about this individual, what would be the next step?

My recommendation is to begin by checking for his name in the index of Emmett Starr's "History of the Cherokee Indians." This book is one of the primary resources to use for tracing Cherokee ancestry, but don't expect all surnames to be in it.

The index shows no Bryant Ward, but it does show several pages containing information on a name spelled Bryan Ward (no "t" on Bryant). A review of these quickly indicates that all are relatives, but one of them, listed on Starr's page 382, is definitely the subject of our search.

It shows "Bryan" Ward as the son of one John Ward and Catherine McDaniel and brother to James, George, Samuel Charles, Elizabeth, Susie, and Nannie Ward; also that his wife's name was Temperance Stansel. Looking back at our roll on page 12, you will note the names of all his brothers listed in the section near his name and that of my grandmothers: James, George, Samuel, and Charles. The Star book indicates that Bryant's sister Susie married a William England, and sister Elizabeth married Elijah Sutton. These names also appear on other pages of that same reservation roll— all but his sister Nannie are accounted for. The name listed as "Caty Ward, a widow," listed immediately above my grandmother's name, is Bryant Ward's mother as confirmed by Starr's book. Under close scrutiny, (not visible in our printed example) it can be seen that the black area in the column to the far right of the role page on the same line as Caty Ward contains a barely visible entry, "Proxy of William England." This, of course, would be her son-in-law, married to Susie.

What else is to be learned here about Bryant (Bryan) Ward from Starr's History? For one thing, it reveals that he fathered at least five children who reached adulthood, because it includes their names and the names of their spouses. Page 468 explains that his mother Catherine (Caty) was of ½ Cherokee blood and that she had married John Ward, the son of a white, English trader named Bryan Ward whose first wife had died (Ward's second wife was Nancy Ward, a full blood of the Wolf Clan also known as the *Ghi-ga-u* or famous Beloved Woman of the Cherokee).

A search of records in the Tennessee State Archives turns up a small booklet entitled *" Springplace: Moravian Mission and The Ward Family Of the Cherokee Nation by Muriel H. Wright."* There, we learn that the mother of our Bryant Ward, Caty McDaniel Ward, was the daughter of a Scottish trader named

McDaniel and his full-blood Cherokee wife named "Granny Hopper," thus we can deduce that Bryant Ward is 1/4 Cherokee.

So, what happened to Bryant Ward after 1817? Did he remain on the Chattahoochee until the time of the Removal and suffer the Trail of Tears? The Cherokee Emigration rolls of 1817-1835 were the next census rolls to be recorded, so to determine his movements, we should check that roll. Sure enough, it contains an entry as roll number 175 and reveals that on March 13, 1832, Bryant Ward of "Little River," Georgia enrolled himself and 6 family members for emigration to the Arkansas Country. A section of the same roll which includes a list of Cherokees who did actually emigrate west of the Mississippi shows that a total of 6 family members, including one male under 50 years of age, one under 25 and one under 10, plus one female under 50 and 2 under 10 arrived in the west on May 16, 1834. They had been removed "in wagons and steamboats by Lt. J.W. Harris" of the U.S. Army. Now we have a second name (Harris) that we'll want to keep an eye out for as we read.

A quick scan of surnames within the indexes of several texts dealing with the Removal turns up listings for both Lt. J.W. Harris and Bryant Ward. One very well known book is "Indian Removal" by noted author Grant Foreman, and we'll use it here to illustrate, because it not only includes interesting genealogical data about Bryant Ward, but it also offers other important references where we can go to learn more about the Removal period.

Most people associate the grief and pathos associated with the Removal of the Five Civilized Tribes to the West with only the *forced* removal period culminating in the Trail of Tears, itself, which occurred in 1838-39. But history records it differently. The cruel and unnecessary suffering of the emigrants extended well before then to when many Cherokees were voluntarily removing their families to the West. The moral responsibility for the lives and comfort of the men, women and children who were the helpless objects of their racially motivated decrees was of no importance whatsoever to a totally insensitive U.S. President, Congress and Administration.

Consider the words of Lt. Harris, a new West Point graduate of the class of1825, recorded in a journal he kept during the trip west when he was assigned to escort a number of Cherokee families (including Bryant Ward's) who were voluntarily emigrating:

"My blood chills even as I write, at the remembrance of the scenes I have gone through today. In the cluster of cedars upon the bluff which looks down upon the Creek and river, and near a few tall chimneys- the wreck of a once comfortable tenement, the destroyer had been most busily at work. Three large families of the poor class are there encamped, and I have passed much of the day with them, and have devoted the larger portion of my cares to their sufferers- but in vain were my efforts; the hand of death was upon them. At one time I saw stretched around me and within a few feet of each other, eight of these afflicted creatures dead or dying. Yet no loud lamentations went up from the bereaved ones here. They were of the true Indian blood; they looked upon the departed ones with a manly sorrow and silently digged graves for their dead and as quietly they laid them out in their narrow beds . . . There is a dignity in their grief which is sublime; and which, poor and destitute, ignorant and unbefriended as they were, made me respect them.

The dead on the sixteenth were "Alex M'Toy, D. Ross child, Bolingers ditto, Richardson's wife , T. Wilson's child, ***William England****, Brewer's child, one of Wm Vann's and three Black Foxes children; all of whom with the exception of Alex M'Toy have been decently buried and his coffin will be in readiness in a few minutes."*

Seven more died on the seventeenth and the same number the next day. Nearly all those afflicted with cholera were either suffering, or just recovering, from measles. The unusual confinement on the boats and privations to which they were not accustomed debilitated a large number of adults, who particularly were revolted by the daily diet of only salt pork which they were not in the habit of eating. Articles of diet such as coffee and sugar that they were accustomed to use in their homes were denied them unless they had money with which to buy them.

Five died on the nineteenth. One of ***Bryant Ward's children died May 1*** *and another the next day. Bob Shelton's child died and was buried on the third."* [From an unpublished journal in the archives of the Office of Indian Affairs, dated May 9, 1834.]

The party in which Bryant Ward's family emigrated included 457 people. By the time Harris left his charges at Dwight Mission in Indian Territories on May 16, 1834, there had been 81 deaths. Of these, 45 were children under ten years of age. Of the members in this party who reached their new "home" alive, nearly one-half died before the end of the year.

The knowledge that Bryant Ward emigrated to the west makes it likely that there will be other documents in spoilations claims, because these people were promised they would be paid for any "improvements" they lost as a result of leaving the east. A timely request to the National Archives brought back the following records that offer more insights into this Ward family and their journey west:

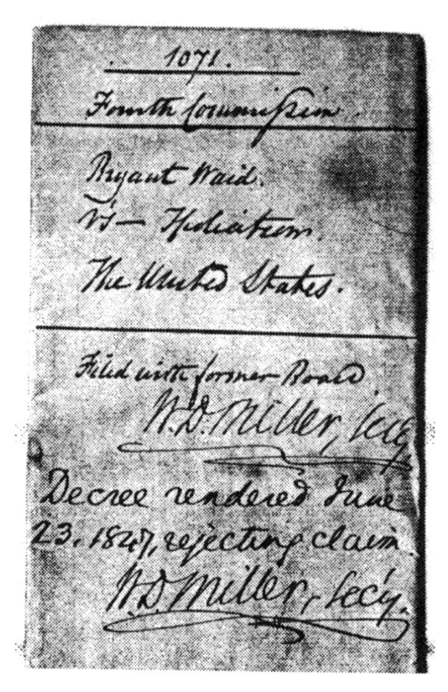
1071.
Fourth Commission
Bryant Ward.
vs — Spoliation.
The United States.
Filed with former Board.
W.D. Miller, Secy
Decree rendered June 23, 1847, rejecting claim.
W.D. Miller, Secy.

I Bryant Ward, the within named Claimant, appeared before the Commissioners and makes the following Statement.

That he is the head of a Cherokee family, Married in the Old Nation within the limits of Georgia in the year of 1818 — I am a Native Cherokee and removed to this Country in the year of 1824, in ~~a detatchment under charge of Lieut Harris~~ We were brought up the Arkansas river on the Steamboat Thomas Yateman — and ran aground at the mouth of the Cadron, some distance above Little Rock — The Agent then put us on shore at that place — and furnished some teams to bring up the party of about 700 in number The wagons could not bring near all our things and they were left on the shore — all the articles charged for in the within account were left by this Claimant and ~~he never received them nor was paid for them afterwards~~ The agent promised that the things should be brought up but it was never done.

I live on Grand river about one hundred miles above Fort Gibson, in the Cherokee Nation — Bryant Ward

Commissioners Office, Fort Gibson March 4th 1840

The above named Bryant Ward appeared before me and made the above Statement.

John T. Mason

A Detatchment of Cherokees Transported by Lieut. Harris United States Army to Arkansas left Calhoun Tennessee the 12th day of March 1834 and arrived at Decadron on or about the 28th day of April of the same year as a Water passage could not obtained any farther than that Point the United States Government employed Wagons to the dissatisfaction of the emigrating party to bring their property to Arkansas which was a great loss to said party owing to the Govt. not permitting the emigrants to bring with them what was theirs. The following statements exhibits a Correct statement of the property of Bryant Ward left a Decadron—

2 Beds and Furniture	50	00
1 Trunk of Shoes 63 pairs at $2.12½ per pair	131	75
1 Cherry Table	3	50
8 Chairs at 75¢ per piece	6	00
2 Large Pots 3.25 per piece	6	50
1 " Oven	2	50
1 Small do	2	75
1 Hand saw	3	00
2 Felling Axes 2.50¢ per piece	5	00
1 Bar Shear Plough	3	00
1 Bull Tongue do	2	00
1 Shovel do	2	00
3 Sets Harness $5 per Set	15	00
3 Weeding Hoes	3	00
2 Smoothing Irons	2	00
3 Chisels & Augurs	3	00
1 Drawing Knife	1	75
	$192	75

river on the Steamboat Thomas Yateman. At the Mouth of a Creek Called Cadron, the Steamboat ran aground and Could get no farther. The Cholera broke out among the Cherokees aboard and we were put a shore. We Knew Mr Ward and his family well in the Old Nation and Knew that he had a quantity of furniture and provisions on the boats. We Can not tell how much he was Compelled to leave but We Knew the wagons Could not bring near all the articles up, that were put ashore. The Agent (Lieut Harris) promised that the articles should be sent up — Mr Ward and his family told us At the time and frequently Since that they had left a great Many articles of furniture and provisions — but we Can not say of our own Knowledge how much. We were all then in trouble and engaged in our own Concerns

Ruth her x mark Mattoy

Betsy her x mark Smith

Commissioners Office, Fort Gibson March 16th 1805, The above Witnesses, Ruth Mattoy and Betsy Smith appeared before me and upon examination, gave the above testimony

John T. Mason

These records reflect that Bryant Ward appeared before the Commissioners and stated: *"I am a Native Cherokee and removed to this country in the year of 1834, in a detachment under charge of Lieut. Harris. We were brought up the Arkansas River on the Steamboat Thomas Yeatman and ran aground at the mouth of the Cadron, some distance above Little Rock - The agent (referring to Lt. Harris) there put us on shore at that place- and furnished some teams to bring up the party of about 700 in number. The wagons could not bring near all our things and they were left on the shore - all the articles charged for in the written account were left by this claimant and he never received them nor was paid for them afterwards. The agent promised that the things should be brought up but it was never done. I live in Grand River about one hundred miles above Fort Gibson, in the Cherokee Nation."*

/s/ Bryant Ward.

Commissions Office Fort Gibson, March 14, 1845

The above named Bryant Ward appeared before me and made the above statement.

/s/ John Tichason.

Attached to the statement is an individual listing of household goods which apparantly represents everything the family owned, showing a total value of $193.75. The statements of two Cherokee women, Ruth Mattoy and Betsy Smith testifying in Ward's behalf are also shown, as is the government's decision -two years later in 1847- denying the claim!

There are numerous other documents to be had which pertain to Mr. Ward such as a will filed in Franklin County Georgia in 1815 before he removed west and records of his death, burial and later reburial due to the construction of a dam that would have inundated the graveyard, just to mention two. All of these records can provide additional clues to the history of his family and, equally important, other surnames.

Remember - one lead almost always leads to several others, and just how much you can find out about the family you are researching depends largely on how much time and effort you are willing to invest. If your relative does not appear on any Cherokee roll to give you a beginning foundation, plan on spending a lot of time mulling over dusty old record books in secluded county courthouses. Fall back on conventional genealogy methods (the same as you would for non-Indian ancestors), roll up your sleeves and go to work.

Don't discount anything; land deeds, bills of sale, court actions, marital records, death records, and voter registrations sometimes contain information important to your search.

Pay particular attention to any locally produced old family histories in your local library and church records in the area where your ancestor lived at any time. All repositories have some of these and they often contain information that you will never find anywhere else... great-great-great's maiden names, etc., and that ever-so-slight, never-again-recorded mention that they were of Indian blood!

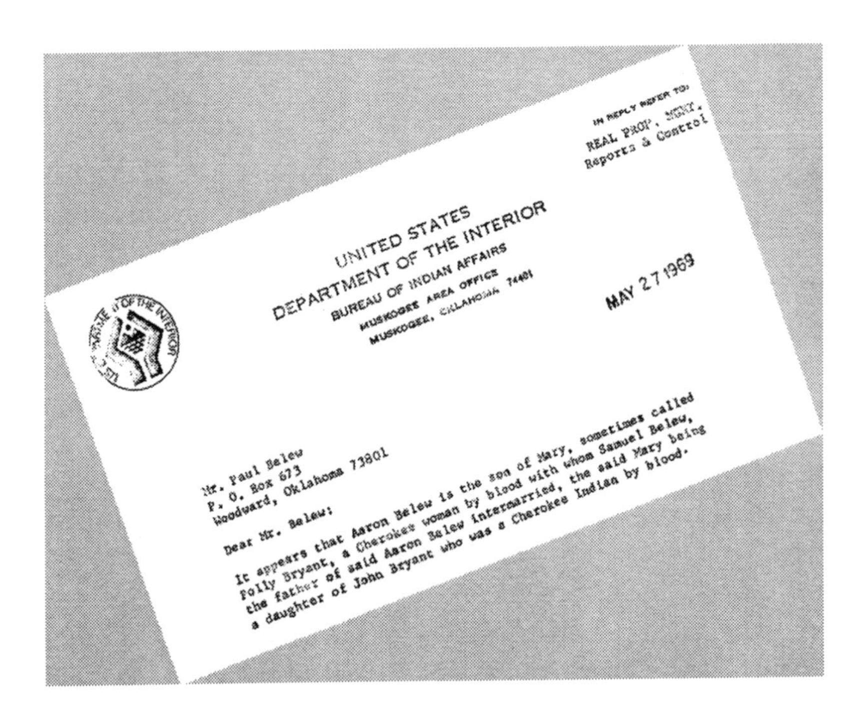

IN REPLY REFER TO:
REAL PROP. MGMT.
Reports & Control

UNITED STATES
DEPARTMENT OF THE INTERIOR
BUREAU OF INDIAN AFFAIRS
MUSKOGEE AREA OFFICE
MUSKOGEE, OKLAHOMA 74401

MAY 27 1969

Mr. Paul Belew
P. O. Box 673
Woodward, Oklahoma 73801

Dear Mr. Belew:

It appears that Aaron Belew is the son of Mary, sometimes called Polly Bryant, a Cherokee woman by blood with whom Samuel Belew, the father of said Aaron Belew intermarried, the said Mary being a daughter of John Bryant who was a Cherokee Indian by blood.

following year returned with their families. During the same year ---- Biggs located about four miles northwest of the present site of Trenton, —— Hughbanks (John Eubanks) settled at a point about six miles west of Dyer. At about the same time, probably in the spring of that year, Colonel David Crockett came from Lawrence County, Tennessee, and located a short distance northeast of Rutherford. In the fall, John Bergin, his brother-in-law, came and with him brought Crockett's family. L. K. Tinkle and H. McWhirter, also brothers-in-law of Colonel Crockett, came soon after, and settled in the same vicinity. Others who settled in the neighborhood of where Rutherford now is were Henry, Jacob, Humphrey and Bryant Flowers, and the Edmundsons: Robert, Allen, Michael and William. A settlement in the vicinity of Yorkville was begun very early by William Holmes, who located two miles south of that place. He was followed by the Reeds—Samuel, James, William, Robert, and Hugh—Benjamin Tyson, Benjamin S. White and John W. Needham. John B. Hogg and Thomas Gibson located on the present site of Trenton. David P. Hamilton, in 1822, began a settlement about two miles east of Humboldt. His early neighbors were Davidson Waddell, William P. Seat, George Gentry, W. G. B. Killingsworth and Alexander G. Hamilton. (In the early thirties Samuel Cole, Thomas Walker and brothers, and others moved from North Carolina into the same community. The village of South Gibson, established by Wm. P. Williams and carried forward by his brothers, Wilson and Thomas J., was the center of this neighborhood).[3] The first settler in the vicinity of Bradford was Richard Smith who, with others, subsequently joined the Mormons at Nauvoo, Ill. The settlement in the vicinity of Lynn Point was made by Robert Puckett, Hiram Partee, Samuel, William, Robert and James Baker, Peter Meyers, Dr. Joseph Dean, Joseph Dibrell, "Rutherford" David Crockett and "Little" David Crockett. The early settlers of Skullbone were William Goodman, William Stone, James Andrews, John Bryant and several sons, Patterson Crockett and John R. Tedford (Thedford?)."[4]

In 1821 when Carroll, Henderson and Madison Counties were established, there was an insufficient number of settlers to establish Gibson County. For this reason the future county was made a ward of Carroll

[3] Williams, *ibid.*

[4] Goodspeed's, *History of Tennessee.*

Partial Page from Gibson County, Past and Present
(Indian Country and the Western Wilds)
by Frederick Culp and Mrs. Robert Ross.
(A locally produced West Tennessee County History mentioning the author's great grandfather John Bryant and Davy Crockett).

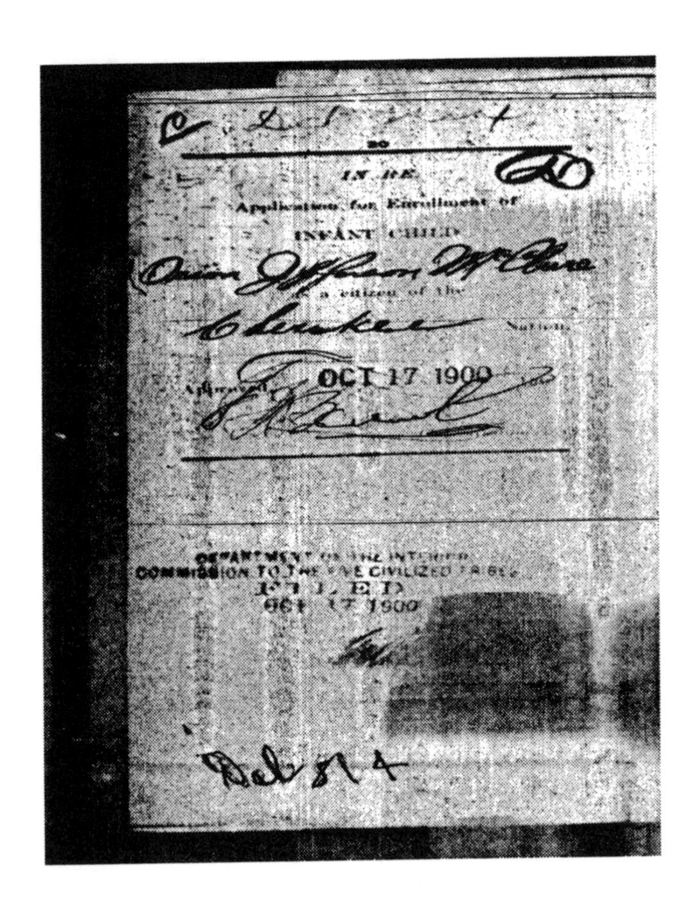

IN RE.

Application for Enrollment of

INFANT CHILD

a citizen of the

Cherokee Nation.

Approved OCT 17 1900

DEPARTMENT OF THE INTERIOR
COMMISSION TO THE FIVE CIVILIZED TRIBES
FILED
OCT 17 1900

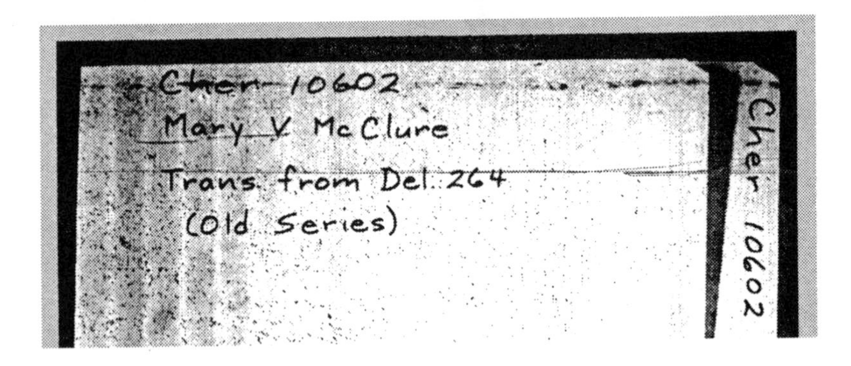

Cher 10602

Mary V McClure

Trans. from Del. 264
(Old Series)

Cher 10602

More National Archives Enrollment Documents from Record Group 75 - Cherokee Nation

Research Notes for Adopted Cherokees

For persons of Cherokee descent who know they are adopted, tracing biological family roots can sometimes be quite a challenge. Legally, birth records are usually sealed until the adoptee is eighteen years of age. After that, in most states, adoptees have legal access to biological family records.

It is always best to try to discuss adoption particulars with adoptive parents first. Attempt to get any information available about tribal affiliation of birth parents and/or their other relatives and the state or region in which you were born. If this information is not available or difficult to obtain, it's a good idea to sign up on adoption registers and not just those associated with Native Americans. Here are some suggestions:

American Indian Adoption Resources Exchange Council of Three Rivers American Indian Center
200 Charles St.
Pittsburgh, PA 15238
Phone 412-782-4457

Adopted and Searching Adoptee Birth Parent Reunion Registry
401 E.74th St.
New York, NY 10021
Phone 212-988-0110

Adoptees and Birth Parents in Search
P.O. Box 5551
West Columbia, SC 29171
Phone 803-796-4508

Adoptees Together
Route 1, Box 30-B-5, Climax, N.C. 27233

National Adoption Information Clearinghouse
11426 Rockville Pike
Rockville, MD 20852

I highly recommend the following two texts which go to the heart of the adoption issue and offer helpful information for Native American adoptees in particular:

Kingsolver, Barbara. ***Pigs in Heaven.*** New York: Harper-Collins, 1989. (This loving book deals with the complexities involved between a mother and her adopted Cherokee daughter and their experiences with the Cherokee Nation of Oklahoma).

Nash, Renea D. ***Coping as a Biracial/Biethnic Teen.*** New York: Rosen Publishing Group, 1995. (Examines some of the dilemmas and special issues involved for teenagers of mixed blood who are attempting to develop their ethnic identity).

In some cases, you can find a living relative by requesting a copy of his or her social security application. This is considered classified information, but the administration can decide whether or not they think release of the information is warranted. Request and complete form SSA-L997. **Social Security Administration, Office of Central Records Operations, Baltimore, MD 21201.**

Over the years I have had a number of friends who were adopted with no idea of who their birth parents are. Naturally, this is a sensitive issue and it is quite normal to be curious about it. Patience and persistence will often pay off, however, so whatever you do, don't ever give up! My good friend, Meg Scraper Howland (*Walks Alone*) of Oceanside, California has spent years searching for her biological roots. She still hasn't discovered who her birth parents were, but through painstaking work, she has recently gained enrollment in the Cherokee Nation of Oklahoma. Bravo to this very special lady and cherished Cherokee sister!

Native Newspapers

Obviously, Indian newspapers can keep you up to date on the latest happenings within Native America- local and other tribal events, health, politics, editorials, education and more. But researchers often overlook the fact that they also sometimes contain a bounty of valuable historical and genealogical information. Some also carry language lessons and other important social issues. There are four Cherokee newspapers:

The Cherokee Advocate is the official monthly newspaper of the Cherokee Nation of Oklahoma. $12.50 annually within Oklahoma, $10 for senior citizens; $15 and $12.50 for seniors outside Oklahoma.// P.O. Box 948, Tahlequah, OK. 74465.

The Cherokee Observer is the only "independent" Cherokee Newspaper. Published monthly; $12.50 annually US, $25.00 outside the US.// P.O. Box 1301, Jay, OK. 74346-1301.

The Cherokee One Feather is published weekly by the Tribal Council of the Eastern Band of Cherokees. $25 year within the US.// P.O. Box 501, Cherokee, NC 28719.

The United Keetoowah Band News is published monthly by the United Keetoowah Band of Cherokee Indians of Oklahoma. $10 annually within the US. // P.O. Box 746, Tahlequah, OK 74465-0746.

The largest Indian newspaper in the United States is **Indian Country Today**, published weekly, and while it's primary focus is the Northern Plains, Northwest, Southwest and Midwest (all tribes), it does contain information of interest to Eastern natives including Cherokees. $58 year U.S. // 1920 Lombardy Drive, Rapid City, SD 57701.

Homeland of the Cherokees . . .
The Great Smoky Mountains
(Photos by the Author)

Enrollment Information

If you are conducting family research with a goal of gaining tribal membership in one of the three federally recognized Cherokee tribes (Western Cherokee Nation or United Keetoowah Band headquarted in Tahlequah Oklahoma or the Eastern Band of Cherokees in Cherokee, Qualla Boundary, North Carolina), it is important to know the following: To register as a member of the Western Cherokee Nation one must prove direct decendancy from a person of Cherokee Blood enrolled by *DAWES* during the period of 1898 to 1914 (An in-depth explanation of this role appeared earlier). Direct descendancy refers to **mother, father, or grand-parents.** Unfortunately, aunts, uncles, brothers etc. DO NOT qualify. Simultaneous applications for "Certificate of Degree of Indian Blood" and "Cherokee Nation Membership" are required. Birth certificates, death certificates, and Court Records are some of the means of proving direct descendancy from a person listed on the DAWES Roll. Note that tribal agencies DO NOT accept Federal Census Records as proof of Indian blood.

It is your burden to prove to the Cherokee Nation that you are entitled to be registered in their community as a member and according to their rules. Regardless of the fact that the DAWES roll was a U.S. Government orchestrated requirement, if your ancestor is not listed on it, you simply won't be allowed to enroll, even if you have positive proof that you are 100 percent Cherokee! Welcome to the world of government bureaucracy.

If your descendant IS listed on the DAWES ROLL, and you desire to attempt enrollment in the Western Cherokee Nation, applications may be obtained from:

Cherokee Nation,
Tribal Register
Tahlequah, OK. 74465
Phone 918-456-0671

Enrollment requirements for the United Keetoowah Tribe and Eastern Band of North Carolina are even more stringent. Until just recently an applicant for enrollment in the eastern band was required to prove direct decendancy from a person who was listed on the Baker Roll of 1924 and have a minimum 1/16 blood quantum.

After Feb 15, 1996, ENROLLMENT IN THE EASTERN BAND WAS RESTRICTED TO NEWBORNS ON THE RESERVATION, however this is always subject to change.

For current information, contact:

Eastern Band of Cherokee Indians
Tribal Enrollment Office
Council House
Cherokee, N.C. 28719

Enrollment in the United Keetoowah Tribe of Oklahoma under UKB Membership Ordinance 90 UKB 9-16, 16 September 1990, provides that any descendant of 1/4 Cherokee Indian blood of any enrollee on the 1949 UKB Base Roll, **or on any other historical Cherokee Roll**, shall be eligible for enrollment in the UKB. Final determination of Cherokee Indian blood quantum rests with the UKB Tribal Council. For applications, call or write:

United Keetoowah Band
of Cherokee Indians of Oklahoma
P.O. Box 746
Tahlequah, Ok. 74465-0746
Phone (918) 456-5491

Over the years, the "rolls rules," have led to the formation of numerous non-federal tribes in various parts of the country. Some of these are officially recognized and chartered by their individual state governments.

You might want to consider membership in the better of these over federal tribes, even if you are qualified for the latter, simply because there is less government interference and control. Just keep in mind that they will be asking what you can do for them, instead of what they can do for you. I also strongly recommend that you check out the credentials, goals, policies and tribal enrollment requirements of any non-federal tribe you consider applying to. The common denominator for authenticity, credibility and approval by state governments seems to be an absolute requirement for proving descendancy from a Cherokee ancestor. The vehicle used by tribes to substantiate this usually is a requirement that applicants prove direct decendancy from an ancestor whose name appears on some roll , but not just the Dawes or Baker Rolls as required by federal tribes. In some instances, certified family documents will be accepted.

Following is a list of known non-federal tribes, some of which have provided enrollment requirements. Their listing here is for informational purposes and should not be construed as an endorsement by the writer unless noted elsewhere in this book:

Cherokee Tribe of Northeast Alabama

(Formerly North Alabama Cherokees)

This is a tribe of over 2000 "bloodline" Cherokee descendants that neither desires nor seeks federal recognition, but is recognized by the State of Alabama Indian Affairs Commission.
No blood quantum requirement, however applicants must be able to trace and document bloodline back to a Cherokee ancestor(s) whose name appears on ANY one of the federal Cherokee rolls.

We have a minimun of four annual festivals (Pow-wows).
For more information and/or applications please contact:

Jim Pell, Principal Chief
P.O. Box 1227
Scottsboro, AL 35768

Southeastern Cherokee Confederacy, Inc

Principal Chief Vivian Lawson

Your acceptance to the SeCCI is NOT conditional that your family names be found on any one of the Cherokee census rolls. You must provide required information with complete family tree along with a notarized, completed application.The Southeastern Cherokee Confederacy Inc. was recognized as a Cherokee Tribal Nation of people by proclamation of the state of Georgia on December 20,1976. There is no blood quantum requirement by the SeCCI and we have a scholarship fund supported entirely by donations.We do not solicit funds nor are there membership dues after a $30 application processing fee. The SeCCI is NOT a church or a club. It is a tribe of Cherokee people who support the culture, history, language and traditions of their Tsalagi elders.
For more information or applications, call 912-879-1325.

Echota Cherokee Tribe of Alabama

The Echota Cherokee tribe is one of the largest tribes of Cherokee in the state of Alabama and recognized by the State of Alabama Indian Affairs Commission.
Principal Chief: Wayne Rasco; P.O. Box 15
Cook Springs, Alabama 35052
For Tribal application information, contact:

Tribal secretary: Darlene Castleberry
P.O. Box 2128
Sylacauga, Al 35150
Anyone wishing to affiliate with the tribe must complete an application and provide the requested proof of their indian heritage. This proof can include any geneologies, family and public records and any signed, notarized affidavits from the oldest living family members testifying to heritage. The Echota accepts members with as little as 1/32 bloodline.

Cherokee of Southeastern Alabama

Deal Wambles
510 S. Park Ave.
Dothan, AL 36301

Cherokee's Of Northern California

P.O. Box 2644
Citrus Heights, CA 95611
Phone: 916-685-3820

Cherokees of California Inc.

Chief: Barbara Little Star Simertoth
P.O. Box 2372
Marysville, CA 95901
Phone: 916-633-4038

Tuscola United Cherokee Tribe of Florida & Alabama, Inc.

H.A. Rhoden
P.O. Box S
Geneva, FL 32732

Amonsoquath Tribe of Cherokee

Chief Sally Timewalker Blackwell
5 North 24th Street
Defuniak Springs, Fl 32433

Free Cherokee National Veterans Band

Chief Lone Wolf Howell
P.O. Box 801
Deland, Fl 32721

Pan American Indian Association

Chief Piercing Eyes David Turnbull
P.O. Box 244
Nocatee, Fl 33864

Cherokees of Georgia, Inc.

Cane Break Band of Eastern Cherokees
Mrs. Maryanna Cain
Route 3 Box 750
Dahlonega, GA 30533
Phone: 404-864-6010

Georgia Tribe of Eastern Cherokees

Mr. Thomas Mote
P.O. Box 993
Dahlonega, GA 30533
Phone: 404-864-3805

Free Cherokee of NW Georgia

Chief Robert T. Murray—Silver Fox
604 Ridgeland Road
Rossville, GA 30741

Chickamauga Cherokee Nation;
Sac River & White River Bands

205 W. 2nd
Fair Play, MO 65490
Phone: 417-654-4003

Amomsoquath Tribe of Cherokee

Chief Walking Bear Wilson
P.O. Box 296
Deering, MO 63840

Northern Cherokee Tribe of Indians

Elva Beltz
P.O.Box 1121
Independence , MO 64051
Phone: 816-461-6540

Northern Chickamauga Cherokee
Nation of AR/MO

Donald Coones
Route 2 Box 2029
Fair Play, MO 65469
Phone: 816-449-5785

Northern Cherokee Nation Of The Old
Louisiana Terrritory

1502 E. Broadway, Suite 201
Columbia, MO 65201

Cherokees of Hoke Co.

Rev. Edgar Bryant
Route 1 Box 129-C
Lumber Bridge, NC 28357
Phone: 919-323-4848

Cherokee Powhattan
Dorothy Crowe
P.O. Box 3265
Roxboro, NC 27573
Phone: 919-599-6448

Cherokees of Robinson & Adjoining Cos.
Mr. Fermon Locklear
Route 2 Box 272-A
Red Springs, NC 28377

The Ohio Cherokees
Chief Oliver Collins
247 Old U.S. Hiwy-52 Unit A
West Portsmouth, OH 45663

**Northwest Cherokee Wolf Band,
Southeastern Cherokee
Confederacy, Inc.**
P.O. Box 592
Talent, OR 97540
Phone: 503-535-5406

Etowah Cherokee Nation
Hugh Gibbs
P.O. Box 5454
Cleveland, TN 37320

**Red Clay Intertribal Band:
S.E. Cherokee Confederacy Inc.**
John Neikirk
7703 Georgetown Road
Ooltewah, TN 37363
Phone: 615-238-9346

Tennessee River Band of Chickamauga Cherokee
Chief Golanv Ahwi Brown
9001 Bill Reed Road
Ooltewah, TN 37363

Free Cherokee Good Medicine Society
Chief Grey Eagle
615 Jolly Road
Grandview, TN 37337

Southeastern Cherokee Tribe & Associated Bands
Chief Charles "Whitedog" Boudreaux
P.O. Box 2001
Porter TX 77368
Phone:713-429-9991

Tsalagiyi Nvdagi/Cherokee in Texas
P.O. Box 492
Troup TX 75789
Chief Utsidihi D.L. Hicks
Phone 903-842-3329

Rocky Mt. Band of Cherokee Decendants
Principal Chief: Larry "War Eagle" Williams
9162 W. Copper Cove Cir.
Magna, UT 84044

Virginia Cherokee Tribe
Chief Sam Penn Sr.
804-845-5606

The Northern Tsalagi Indian Nation
Principal Chief: Vivian Santini
Route 3 Box 1941
Evington, VA 24550

United Cherokee Tribe of WV, Inc.
Chief Bernard Humbles/Penn
123 Turkeyfoot Road
Sewickly, PA 15143

A Brief History of The Cherokee People

Wars with the Iroquois tribes of the New York area and the Delaware tribes pushed the early Cherokees southeast to the Allegheny and Appalachian mountain regions in modern North and South Carolina, Tennessee, northern Georgia and Alabama.The Spanish explorer Hernando de Soto encountered them about 1540 and by this time they had an advanced, agricultural eastern woodland culture. In 1715, smallpox reduced their population by half to about 11,000.

During the British and French struggle for control of colonial North America, and during the American Revolution, the Cherokee generally sided with the British. British goods, especially firearms, were important in keeping the Cherokees a powerful nation. British traders settled among the Indians, took Indian wives, and produced mixed-blood families. Soon, names like Rogers, Adair, Ward, Vann, and Ross began to appear as prosperous merchants, traders, planters, teachers, writers and diplomats within the tribe.

In 1785 they negotiated a peace treaty with the United States, but Cherokee resistance continued for a decade afterwards. In 1791 a new treaty reconfirmed the earlier one; portions of Cherokee land were ceded to the United States, and so-called "permanent rights" of the tribe to the remaining territory were established.

About 3000 tribal members, rightfully disgruntled about the continued encroachment of their territory by white settlers, migrated west of the Mississippi between 1790 and 1817. They first settled in southeast Missouri and then moved to northwest Arkansas. In later years, these would become the first members of what was eventually known as the Western Band.

Cherokee economy, like that of the other southeastern tribes, was based on intensive agriculture, mainly corn, beans, and squash. They hunted deer, bear and elk. The Busk, or Green Corn Ceremony, was a time of thanksgiving, rekindling of sacred fires, and spiritual renewal. The tribe was divided into seven matrilineal clans, or families, dispersed in war and peace moieties (half-tribes). The marriage of persons belonging to the same clan, and of the father's clan was strictly forbidden; also marriage was prohibited between relatives by blood. The penalty for breaking this law was capital punishment. The mother was the head of the family and the children were called by the name of her clan. People lived in many permanent villages, some of which belonged to the war moiety, the rest to the peace moiety. They believed in one God or "Great Spirit," but they also believed in witch-craft and conjurers. Conjurors were doctors who not only cured diseases but were thought to have the power to counteract the evil doings of witches.

In the early 19th century, the Cherokee demonstrated unusual adaptability to Western institutions, both in their governmental changes and in their adoption of western methods of animal husbandry and farming, including the plantation system. In 1820 the tribe established a Republican governmental system modeled on that of the United States, with an elected principal chief, a senate, and house of representatives. Because of this system, the Cherokee were recognized as one of the "Five Civilized Tribes." In 1827 they drafted a constitution and incorporated as the Cherokee Nation. Public schools were established and in the 1820's, Sequoyah (also known as George Guess), a tribal member, invented an 85-character syllabary for the Cherokee language. Widespread literacy followed almost immediately. In 1828 the first Native American newspaper, the *Cherokee Phoenix*, was established by Elias Boudinot (Buck Watie).

Valuable gold deposits were discovered in tribal lands in 1828, which by previous cessions had been reduced to about 7 million acres in northwest Georgia, eastern Tennessee, and southwest North Carolina. Georgia appealed to the U.S. government to remove the Cherokee from Georgia lands. When the appeal failed, attempts were made to purchase the territory. In retaliation the Cherokee Nation enacted a law forbidding any such sale on punishment of death. In 1828 the Georgia legislature outlawed the Cherokee government, confiscated tribal lands and also made it illegal for an Indian to testify against whites in court. The Cherokee, realizing this would allow white settlers to seize their lands at will, brought suit. Their appeals for federal protection were rejected by President Andrew Jackson. In 1832 the Supreme Court of the United States ruled that the Georgia legislation was unconstitutional, but federal authorities, following Jackson's insane, racial policy of Native American removal, ignored the decision.

Internal division within the tribes saw a few leaders in favor of removing to the west with the majority preferring to remain on their ancestral lands. Still, it gave the white expansionists a valuable opening to exploit. After relentless harassment by the Jackson administration and Georgia authorities, and the inability of the Supreme Court to enforce its decisions, a handful of leading Cherokee agreed in an illegal treaty (New Echota Treaty of 1835) to cede all tribal land in exchange for $5,700,000 and land in Indian Territory (now Oklahoma). Their action was repudiated by more than nine-tenths of the tribe, and although leaders in Washington were made fully aware of this by their own officials in Georgia, the fraudulent treaty was ratified. When most of the tribe refused to abide by federally mandated removal orders, over 7,000 federal troops and 2,000 state militiamen began forcibly evicting the Cherokee in 1838. Men, women and

Western Cherokee Nation Capitol and Courthouse 1829 - 39 (Indian Territories)

children were taken at gunpoint from their homes, placed in filthy stockades and their belongings left to be plundered by greedy white squatters and Georgia Militiamen.

Some avoided arrest and escaped to the North Carolina mountains and other nearby states, but most of the tribe was taken from the stockades and driven west to Indian Territories in a twelve hundred mile forced march in the dead of winter. This infamous trek would become known to the Indian as *"Nunahi-Duna-Dio-Hilu-I," or "Trail Where They Cried."* Others refer to it as *"The Trail of Tears*. Of approximately 16,000 men, women and children who were so removed, about 4000 perished through hunger, disease, and exposure.

In Indian Territory, three well known signers of the bogus treaty that had ceded eastern lands in the New Echota treaty were savagely assassinated. This triggered destructive civil strife, but eventually the factions fused. In 1839.the Cherokees reorganized their government and adopted a new constitution under their same principal chief, John Ross. Tahlequah was chosen as their national capitol and mission schools were set up throughout the nation. Male and Female Seminaries were opened in 1851.

During the American Civil War, most of the tribe sided with the Confederacy, however the Blackhawk Keetowah factions supported the Union. The nation became a battleground for both armies, and in the summer of 1862, Tahlequah was occupied by Union forces.

After the war, old differences resurfaced and the healing process was slow. The planter class of mix-bloods, many of whom had become wealthy, educated, and receptive to all the Victorian attitudes of the corresponding stratum in southern white society was set apart from its full-blood tribesmen by formidable barriers. English became its first language, evangelical Christianity its religion, and acculturation its code. The homes and improvements of tribesmen had been destroyed; their fields and ranches desolated by four years of wasteful war.Unfortunately, they were unable to present a united front to thwart another coming upheaval.

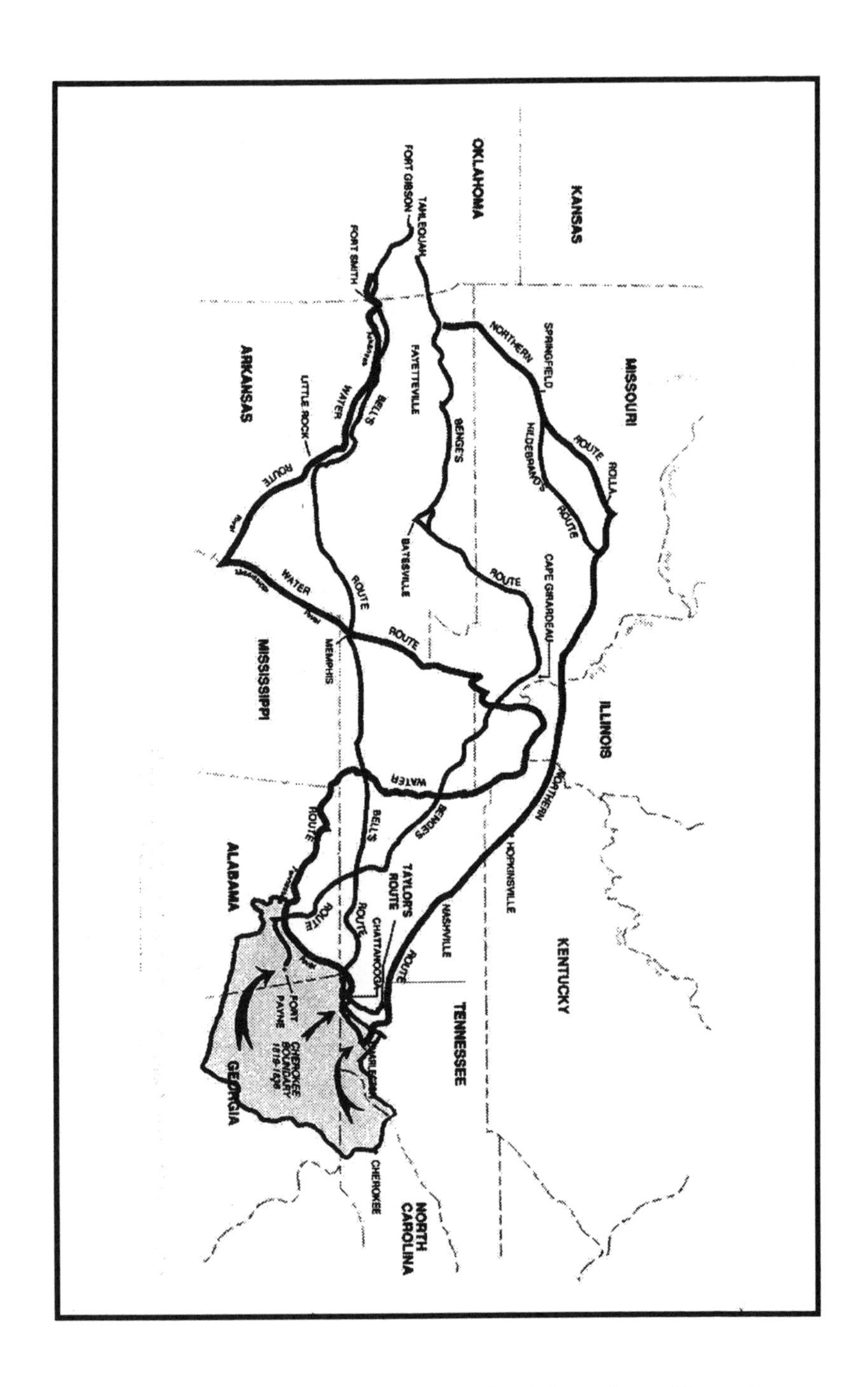

Land and Water Routes Used During Cherokee Removal to Indian Territories in the West.

Under the General Allotment Act of 1887—uncompromisingly resisted by the Cherokee—plots of tribal land were forcibly allotted to individual members. The government of the Cherokee Nation was dissolved, and its people became U.S. citizens when Oklahoma achieved statehood in 1907. Surplus lands were parceled out by the federal government, and in 1891 the tribe's western land extension, the Cherokee Strip or Cherokee Outlet, was sold to the United States. In 1893 it was opened, mostly to white settlers, in a famous land run. One more treaty between the U.S. politicians and the Cherokee People had been broken (according to he preamble of the treaty of 6 May 1828, the Cherokee people, upon removal to the west, would *"never in all furture times . . . be pressed upon by the extension...of any existing Territory or State...* Of a total of 40 such treaties, each and every one has been broken by the United States Government!

Back east, some tribesmen who escaped to the mountains and avoided the Trail of Tears remained there, although the 1835 treaty had divested them of their lands. Pressure to force their removal continued. Many alienated themselves from the rest of their tribesmen and dispersed to other parts of the southeast, never to return.Those who remained in North Carolina became subject to the laws of that state even though they were not admitted to citizenship. Because they steadfastly refused to remove to the Western IndianTerritories, monies due them under treaty obligations were withheld by the government unless they could succeed in getting permission from the North Carolina government to remain there.

In 1866, the North Carolina legislature approved a statute granting the Cherokees the right to stay in that state. Secretly, they had already begun a systematic purchase of lands through a white agent named Will Thomas, and when it finally became legal for Indians to own land, he transferred ownership to the tribe, as promised. After numerous lawsuits, these lands were eventually placed in trust to the U.S. Government for the Eastern Cherokees as a corporation.

Today, tribal corporate lands owned by the Eastern Band comprise almost 57,000 acres scattered over five counties of the area known as Qualla Boundary near the North Carolina and Tennessee state lines. All of it is held in common by the tribe with possession of tracts issued to individuals. Farming, forestry, factory work, and tourism (about 5 million tourists annually) make up the primary sources of income. In 1996, the tribe was granted approval to open a new gaming casino which is expected to increase tourist traffic - and jobs- tremendously. There are about 10,000 tribal members with 8,000 living on tribal lands.

Throughout the United States, Cherokee language has about 10,000 modern speakers and on the 1990 United States Census, 308,132 people listed themselves as Cherokee descendants. Theoretically, due to more than two centuries of inter-marriage, the actual number of people who possess some degree of Cherokee blood probably runs into the millions.

A Prophecy . . .

Where now are our grandfathers. the Delawares? We had hoped the white men would not be willing to travel beyond the mountains. Now that hope is gone. They have passed the mountains. and have settled upon Cherokee land. They wish to have that usurpation sanctioned by treaty. When that is gained. the same encroaching spirit will lead them up on other land of the Cherokees. New cessions will be asked. Finally the whole country. which the Cherokees and their fathers have so long occupied. will be demanded. and the remnant of the Ani-Yunwiya. 'The Real People'. once so great and formidable. will be compelled to seek refuge in some distant wilderness. There they will be permitted to stay only a short while. until they again behold the advancing banners of the same greedy host. Not being able to point out any further retreat for the miserable Cherokees. the extinction of the whole race will be proclaimed. Should we not therefore run all risks. and incur all consequences. rather than submit to further laceration of our country? Such treaties may be all right for men who are too old to hunt or fight. As for me. I have my young warriors about me. We will have our lands.

Dragging Canoe
Cherokee, 1768

Group of distinguished Cherokees negotiating a treaty in Washington, in 1866. Left to right: John Rollin Ridge, Saladin Watie, Richard Fields, Col. Elias C. Boudinot, Col. William P. Adair.

[Cherokee National Historical Society Photograph]

Honoring Your Native Ancestors

It is my personal opinion that every Cherokee descendant has a moral obligation to respect and honor their distinguished heritage, and to make a definitive effort to pass the tradition on to future generations. Since the first foreigner set foot on Native American soil where our people had lived since time immemorial, there has been a concerted effort by some to assimilate all Native Americans into the dominant race; to portray them, at best, as inferior human beings, and purge all traces of their customs and beliefs. As mentioned earlier, attitudes are slowly changing, but the very idea of a "different" people with a different culture living among them still is unacceptable to many, even though they are well aware that, in many cases, the land they live on today was stolen from native people.

At the time of the expulsion of the Cherokee people from their native homelands in the southeast, they were not itinerant barbarians as the government leaders of the day would have us believe. Instead, most were a settled people developing constitutional governments, establishing churches and schools, and farming by usual frontier standards. In the words of Grant Foreman, the Dean of American Indian Historians:

"They loved their streams and valleys, their hills, their forests, their fields and herds, their homes and firesides, families and

friends; they were rooted to the soil. The trees that shaded their homes, the cooling spring that ministered to every family, friendly watercourses, familiar trails and prospects, busk grounds, and council houses were their property and their friends; these simple possessions filled their lives; their loss was cataclysmic."

Unfortunately, we cannot miraculously change the cruel and unnecessary hardships suffered upon our forebears, but it would be both unthinkable and immoral for us not to do everything in our power to remember, honor and respect them.

This is not meant to imply that you should abruptly change your lifestyle and show up at work tomorrow sporting buckskins and moccasins. There are many ways to pay homage and express your pride, depending on individual circumstances.

Becoming enrolled in a reputable tribe and regularly taking part in their organized cultural events is admirable and desirable for some, but time constraints and distance understandably prevents this for others.

Showing a genuine interest by acquiring a reasonably good understanding of Cherokee history can, in itself, be a means of memorial. Armed with this, you will be surprised at the myriad ways you can contribute to perpetuating the remembrance of your ancestors. Civic groups, schools, and especially organizations like the Boy and Girl Scouts will be quick to enlist you to help them learn about Cherokee life and culture. Others tracing their own native ancestors will seek you out to share the benefits of your experience.

There are a number of very worthwhile organizations dedicated to preserving and furthering Cherokee tradition in which you can provide needed financial support, either by membership fees or donations, or if your funds are limited, most also welcome volunteer workers for a variety of beneficial projects.

The Trail of Tears Association is a non-profit corporation working in a cooperative agreement with the National Park Service to protect, promote and preserve two of the routes taken by the Cherokee people during their removal and catastrophic journey to the west. Their goals include promoting awareness of the trail's legacy, including the effects of the U.S. Government's Indian Removal Policy on the Cherokees and other tribes. Assistance and support are needed from individuals and groups who wish to learn, educate others and preserve this important part of Native history. Charter memberships (available only for a limited time) are $15.00 per year and are tax deductible. Contact them at: 1100 N. University, Suite 133, Little Rock, AR 72207-6344.

The Cherokee National Historical Society operates The Cherokee Heritage Center which includes the Museum and bookstore, Tsalagi Theatre and Rural Museum Village at Tahlequah, Oklahoma. Their fine efforts to perpetuate the educational and cultural activities of the Cherokee people are indispensable. Supporting memberships at various levels from Youth ($5 annually) to regular ($30 annually) to Charter Archives benefactors are available: CNHS, P.O. Box 515, Tahlequah, OK 74465, Phone 918-456-6007.

The Cherokee Cultural Society of Houston is a non-profit group dedicated to building community, preserving Cherokee heritage, perpetuating Cherokee Culture and building the future of the Cherokee people. Volunteers produce the *Cherokee Messenger* newsletter which includes news articles, family histories, poetry, recipes and other items of interest. Annual membership dues are $20: Address: P.O. Box 1506, Bellaire, TX 77402-1506, Phone 713-668-9998.

National Museum of the American Indian, a part of the Smithsonian Institution, was created by a Congressional Act in 1989. It is the first national museum to be run by an American Indian and, upon completion, will house the finest collection of native artifacts in the world. Their stated purpose is to change forever the way people view Native Peoples of this hemisphere...to correct misconceptions, to end prejudice, to stop injustice and to demonstrate how Indian cultures are enriching the world. Numerous membership categories are available. For more information, write: NMAI, National Campaign, Smithsonian Institution, Washington, D.C. 20560.

Many states have non-profit organizations designed to provide a number of services to it's Native American citizens. The most popular of these in my own home state of Tennessee is shown here and I urge you to search for and support similar organizations in your area:

Native American Indian Association of Tennessee conducts and promotes seminars, institutes, educational programs and public information activities to raise the level of consciousness of the non-Indian population in the state of Tennessee to a fuller awareness of the past history and current status of Native American Indians. They also sponsor, promote and provide social services and other forms of assistance to American Indians who are in need and locate public and private agencies that can provide health, education, welfare, employment and other services. Membership fees are $10 annually and they do accept tax deductible contributions. NAIA, 211 Union St., Nashville, TN 37201.

The American Indian College Fund raises funds from the private sector primarily for scholarships, the most pressing and immediate need. With the help of a challenge grant from the National Endowment for the Humanities, AICF is building a Native Studies Endowment to maintain and strengthen Native studies programs at each of the colleges. Through a volunteer public education campaign, AICF works to increase public awareness of values and traditions of tribal cultures as well as the higher education needs of Native Americans. For information on how you can take part: AICF, 1111 Osage St., Bldg D, Suite 205A, Boulder, CO 80204.

The Native American Rights Fund is a non-profit legal organization devoted to defending and promoting the legal rights of all Indian people. NARF attorneys, most of whom are native Americans, defend tribes who otherwise cannot bear the financial burden of of obtaining justice in the courts in the United States. It focuses on guaranteeing that national and state governments live up to their legal obligations mainly through work in the courtroom. Here, NARF invokes laws enacted by these same government bodies to give strength and substance to promises that have been empty for too many years. Overall, this emphasis helps individual Native Americans advance toward controlling their own destinies and assuring their own survival. Contact them by telephone at 303-447-8760. Donations are tax deductible.

Mrs. Edith Manor of Brazoria, Texas
The author's eldest maternal Cherokee relative.

When the Memories of Your Loved Ones are Dishonored, Do Something!

One of the most important things you can do as an individual or as a family to honor those who came before you is to stand up and be counted when issues arise that affect either the well being or consciences of any Native People. It has been my experience that few people are willing to express opinions that differ from the prejudices of their social environment, but change comes about only when enough people do something about obvious injustices that occur. Discussing displeasures only in private, being complacent or waiting for someone else to do it simply doesn't work! Letter writing campaigns and phone calls to elected officials, lectures to local groups, and voicing your outrage about insensitive actions on the part of anyone to local print media and radio and television station representatives can work if enough people will just do it.

A good example of the type of event I'm talking about here is illustrated in the following adaptation of a guest editorial about Andrew Jackson that appeared under my byline in numerous newspapers, including *Indian Country Today*, the nation's largest Indian newspaper. How it fits as a means of openly "honoring" your beloved ancestors should become quite obvious....

(Article Reprinted in one of it's Newspaper Forms)

Andrew Jackson:
Hero or Hatchet Man?

by
Tony Mack (McClure), Ph.D.

The often apathetic attitudes of the Tennessee State Historic Society are showing again. Newspapers across Tennessee recently carried a publicity release touting a soon-to-be-released commemorative United States stamp that will feature Nashville's famous equestrian statue of Andrew Jackson superimposed in front of the Tennessee capitol building.

Tennessee Governor Don Sundquist, U.S. Postmaster General Marvin Runyon, U.S. Senator Bill Frist, Martha Ingram, Chairman of the Tennessee 200 Bicentennial Commission, and other state officials unveiled the stamp design on the steps of the Tennessee Capitol building last week. In Runyon's words, *"Here, the character of the people have joined to create a national treasure,"* and he goes on to hail Jackson's spirit as *"valiant"*.

Governor Sundquist saw fit to add, *" This is a worthy symbol of that celebration* [referring to Tennessee's bicentennial, the event the stamp is supposed to comemmorate] *and a fitting tribute to Tennessee and her people."*

Once again, they are asking the citizens of America, who are finally beginning to realize that much of the history heralding some of our predecessors as great heros was really nothing more than hogwash, to pay homage to "*Old Hickory.*" Will they never learn that in deciding whom our real heros are; indeed, who we would like to see "commemorated," as such , most of us have finally become intelligent and caring enough to weigh the effects of one's crimes against the effects of their virtues?

No one can dispute that Andrew Jackson was an elected President of the United States. His accomplishments, though questionable, as a leader in the battle of New Orleans also are well recorded. But also written in those annals of our time are indisputable facts which confirm that he was guilty of bribery, fraud, blatant racism and possibly murder! Do the decision makers in Nashville honestly believe we should simply ignore these attributes in choosing our heros? Or are they just having yet another laugh behind our backs because they are able, time and again, to brainwash us into revering whomever they choose. If this seems ridiculous, consider that as recently as two years ago, Tennessee's highly acclaimed "Tennessee Treasures" traveling museum featured Jackson as its main attraction, and that for decades every twenty-dollar bill in your paycheck has carried his portrait!

Andrew Jackson a murder? Decide for yourself after considering some well-documented facts: By virtue of a fraudulently acquired treaty which Jackson himself orchestrated, he pushed the *Indian Removal Act of the 1830's* through Congress. The results of this obviously immoral and unethical act may well exceed in weight of grief and pathos any other passage in American history; even the well-known exile of the Arcadians falls far behind it in its record of death and misery.

The law required the removal of native Cherokees from the very lands where their ancestors lay buried. Those who did not comply voluntarily were forced to do so. General Winfield Scott's army troops, armed with rifles and bayonets, searched out every remote cabin in the Cherokee country of the great Smoky mountains to seize and bring in all occupants. Families at the dinner table were startled by the sudden appearance of unexpected, armed intruders into their homes who drove them with blows and swearing along weary miles of footpaths that led to hastily built stockades. They arrested men at work in their fields of corn; they dragged women from their spinning wheels and small children from their play. It was common, according to published testimonials, that as these terrified people glanced back for one last look at their paltry, but cherished holdings, they saw their shelters in flames - fired by white settlers who followed on the heels of the soldiers, uncontested, to loot and pillage their cattle, stock, and other meager, personal belongings. Even graves were searched and robbed of valuables deposited with the dead.

According to statements in the military archives, one soldier whom they had assigned to this disgusting task stated years later, *"I fought through the civil war and have seen men shot to pieces and slaughtered by thousands, but the Cherokee Removal was the cruelest work I ever knew."*

A full century before the world would know the hate and greed of a race led by a man named Adolph Hitler, a comparative *ethnic cleansing* had begun right here in our Southeastern mountains . . .in the land of the free. A strategic expurgation of the impure from the midst of the pure, in the settler's eyes, identical to what would later ensue in a far away place called Bosnia.

From October 1838 through March 1839, which encompassed the cruelest months of winter, a grim, forced march of an entire nation was ordered. In an attempt to weather the 1200-mile journey from their familiar homelands in the Tennessee and Georgia Mountains to designated anomalous territories in Eastern Oklahoma, more than 4,000 men, women and children perished from hunger, disease and exposure. The single blanket and paltry salt-pork rations that government agents had issued them proved insufficient to sustain life for many, especially the sick, the aged, and small children who already were ill-prepared for such an odyssey. Thus, the lamentable *Trail of Tears* became one of the most shameful blights in the history of humankind and should have forever stamped a mutation into the reputation of Andrew Jackson, one of Tennessee's favorite sons, and all who had a part in it.

In the words of John Burnett, A U.S. Army interpreter during the forced march, *"Murder is murder . . .Somebody must explain the four-thousand silent graves that mark the trail of the Cherokees to their exile."* Yet, it is 1996, over a century and a half later; no one has ever explained, and today we face still another insult. We are to witness the memories of the men, women and children who died so needlessly at Jackson's hand further desecrated by the issuance of a United States Commemorative stamp that features him!

It is commonly known that attitudes are slow to change and it is no wonder, considering the insensitivities of so many. In a recent reprint series in several southeastern newspapers entitled "History" by historians John Hedge Whitfield and S.C. Williams, one article headlined *History: Settlers Strike Hard at the Cherokees* is an account of white reprisals that followed the "Cherokee invasion" of the Holston and Watauga settlements of Tennessee during the Revolutionary period. The author ends his commentary with the statement:

" It should be a matter of pride to all Tennesseans to know that so many inhabitants of the Tennessee Country played important parts in the war with the Cherokees."

It seems totally incongruous that in an era of bicentennial celebration for the state of Tennessee and so many years after the infamous *"Trail of Tears"* tragedy that an official state historical society or individual historians would dare have the impudence to suggest that we should be proud of the atrocities that any of our European ancestors inflicted upon the native Americans (in this case, the Cherokees) who rightfully occupied this land we now call Tennessee. These so called "settlers' or "early pioneers" were in fact intruders who immorally and unlawfully invaded the ancestral lands of an Indian nation who resided here long before those instruments we know as the Constitution and Bill of Rights were even thought of. Incredibly, even the name "Tennessee" belonged to the Cherokees, as it is an adaptation from their language!

Only after all peaceful pleas for recognition of their rights failed; only after their villages were attacked and their citizens maimed and murdered did the Cherokees retaliate with force against the repeated intrusions. From that day forward in history, the Cherokees have been largely regarded as savages. Even the writings that recorded the conflicts tend to confirm this; they were *"great victories"* if the settlers won, but *"massacres"* when the Indians prevailed.

Regrettably, there are still those among us, especially historical institutions and politicians, who insist on perpetuating the myths about what actually happened in those days, and relentlessly imposing on us, our children and their children, gross misrepresentations about the heroism and greatness of some participants.

Are we to simply totally disregard other wicked and inexcusable criminal acts of Andrew Jackson during his presidency: refusing to allow antislavery phamphlets to be distributed in the U.S. Mail; refusing to carry out his lawful duties as President by refusing to enforce Supreme Court rulings when the state of Georgia violated Native American rights on territories guaranteed by federal treaties; or his destabilization of the nation's currency by transferring taxpayer's monies out of the Bank of the United States into "pet" banks to give more aid and comfort to wealthy bankers loyal to him?

Will it never end? Have Americans reached such a state of low self esteem with callous , "I don't give a damn if it doesn't affect me attitudes," that we are willing to allow the continuation of this brainwashing forever?

The inexcusable treatment of Native Americans throughout the history of this entire country is well recorded and equally as tragic. Besides the nefarious Cherokee "Removal," the Sand Creek, Sappa Creek and Wounded Knee massacres by the U.S. Army serve as just three more shameful examples of almost 400 years of unrelenting savagery against the indigenous people of

America, the most genocidal action by one race against another in the history of man. Even the World War II holocaust in which seven million Jews were exterminated by the Germans doesn't begin to compare with what was done more slowly to Native Americans by American "settlers" and the United States Army. Soldiers and "settlers," we remind you, that still today, *they tell us we should be proud of?*

Obviously, we cannot and should not live in the past. Nevertheless, it is only right that our country should forever bear the disgrace and suffer the retribution of its wrongdoing. We should forgive the responsible parties, but we must never, ever forget! If there is to ever be a complete healing process, instead of taking pride in the atrocities committed by our forebears, we should do everything possible to insure that such brutal, inhumane, criminal acts never happen again. Dispelling delusions which suggest that any of these people had any right whatsoever to do what they did is a first step. And refusing to recognize the perpetrators as "valiant" patriots in any form is a profound responsibility that we all share.

Prevarications of this type will never be corrected until we as individuals have the guts to stand up and say, "NO MORE," when we realize that, by today's standards, one of our so-called heroes would be considered little more than a thug. So what if he was president or governor or whatever. Right is right and wrong is wrong, even if the man did hold the highest office in the land! Is it not inherently wrong either to believe or say what is popular just to satisfy our peers, when in our hearts we know that something is morally or ethically wrong? And don't you agree that passing this garbage on to our children, generation after generation after generation is unforgivable?

In an effort to understand how men like Andrew Jackson and others of that time thought, indeed how incredulously some people still think, it might be enlightening to consider this information gleaned from highly respected Native American Journalist Tim Giago: Five days after the perfidious Wounded Knee Massacre of 1890 in which 300 unarmed men, women and children of the Lakota nation were murdered by the U.S. Army, L. Frank Baum, in his newspaper, the *Aberdeen South Dakota Saturday Pioneer* wrote:

"The Pioneer(newspaper) has before declared that our only safety depends upon the total extermination of the Indians. Having wronged them for centuries we had better, in order to protect our civilization, follow it up by one more wrong and wipe these untamed and untamable creatures from the face of the earth."

Ironically, ten years after penning this dispassionate editorial, this same man who seriously advocated the genocide of an entire race of Americans while publicly admitting that it was wrong, wrote one of the most widely acclaimed children's classics of all time. It was called "*The Wonderful Wizard of Oz.*"

So, wolves in sheep's clothing are all about us. Nevertheless, we still seem to exhault them as heroes and partake of their wares, even when we are fully aware of their vices! Surely, sufficient time has passed and enough learning has taken place for attitudes like this to change. Yet, so long as "respected historians," history books, influential government officials and historical organizations still can convince enough of us to take pride in the treacherous acts of our forefathers and to recognize them as great statesmen, man's inhumanity to man is destined to continue.

Was Andrew Jackson really a hero or was he a hatchet man? Regardless of your race, can you explain to your children why a man who committed such despicable horrors should be honored today on commemorative stamps, with publically displayed statues, in mobile museums, on the nation's money. . . or anywhere else in this country? Think about it.

The Eastern Band of Cherokee Indians

The Honorable Joyce C. Dugan, Principal Chief
The Honorable Gerard Parker, Vice-Chief

February 15, 1996

Tony Mack McClure
434 Distribution Parkway
Collierville, Tennessee 38017

Dear Mr. McClure,

Thank you for your work of January 29, 1996 regarding the "Tennessee Bicentennial Stamp Design". It is disheartening to see a design which so clearly overlooks the important contributions Native Americans have made to the state of Tennessee. Andrew Jackson is controversial and his actions as President are often interpreted as "valiant", a fact, which has offended Native people, myself included.

The words you so eloquently put to paper are feelings shared by the Cherokee community. As a Cherokee leader, I feel we must work together to correct these myths perpetuated by professional historians and politicians. Finding the best method to convey this message of disapproval is the challenge we face. I will pursue a variety of avenues to address the concerns of Native People and also the people of Tennessee. The first is to inform the Cherokee Nation of Oklahoma and the Five Civilized Tribes which were affected by Jackson's removal policy. I will also work to insure a more accurate historical account of the Removal Policy is portrayed in Museums, Historical Societies and publications through our division of Cultural Resources. The frustrations from this type of misrepresentation

Qualla Boundary • P.O. Box 455 • Cherokee, N.C. 28719
Telephone: (704) 497-2771 or 497-4771
Telefax: (704) 497-2952

of the facts must force us to action within our
communities but must also provide us with the
strength to attempt positive change.

Letters and writings such as yours strengthen
my resolve that the Cherokee community has many
friends and supporters. Through this network
we can affect positive change. I hope your writing
receives the public attention it deserves. Your
concerns are shared and I shall do all within
my power to rectify this situation.

With kind regards, I am

Sincerely,

EASTERN BAND OF CHEROKEE INDIANS

Joyce C. Dugan

Joyce C. Dugan
Principal Chief

Some Advice on Recognition

Once you have learned about your Cherokee ancestors and documented the lineage, you might be quite content to simply savor the knowledge and silently pay homage in a private way. This, of course, is a matter of personal choice, but as mentioned earlier, many people will want to take a more active part. If so, can you expect to be accepted by other Cherokees with open arms? With some exceptions to be noted, the extent of recognition is largely up to you, and a few personal words of advice are offered.

It is important to keep in mind that the mayhem and discrimination of the past have not deterred the Cherokee from being an extremely proud and determined people. They are intensely protective and conscientious of the images portrayed of them by anyone, and are particularly watchful of those who claim Cherokee heritage.

Rest assured that if you show up at Big Cove on the Qualla Boundary professing to the locals that your grandmother was of Cherokee royalty, they will quickly dub you a "wannabee," regardless of your ancestry. If you insist on dressing in Kevin Costner costumes when you attend official Cherokee functions, or when visiting predominant Cherokee communities, you will not want to hear the whispers that are sure to ensue. If you use the fact that your distant grandmother was a Cherokee to justify setting yourself up as some kind of shaman or to operate sweat lodges for hire on some secluded farm, have no doubts - your actions will be highly frowned upon. And, if you obviously know little or nothing about Cherokee history or culture, your authenticity is sure to be seriously questioned. Rightly so!

The terms "newager" and "wannabee" are heard a lot more nowadays than a few years ago, largely due to the actions of a few who exploit native culture with only profit motivations. Most of the people who practice these scams have no Indian blood at all, but this isn't always the case. Unfortunately, this sort of activity often results in the unjust stereotyping by some Cherokee Nation citizens of everyone not living within a recognized Cherokee community or possessing a federal tribal enrollment card. This is sad, particularly for bonafide Cherokee descendants whose only impetus is to show respect for their antecedents, profess pride in being of Cherokee blood, and to carry this noble heritage forward to future generations.

Genuine Cherokee descendants find no fault with dubbing those who are frauds as such, and most agree that using ancestry - real or otherwise - for exploitation is unforgivable. Nevertheless, the feelings of those who have no such intentions should also always be considered. Many Cherokee descendants, myself included, want no part of federal recognition or the benefits offered by it under any circumstances, but this should have no bearing whatever on our authenticity. This does not mean that we have less respect for those who are federally recognized, but our preference to follow the ways of our ancestors who chose to avoid government enrollment also should not reflect on our acceptance or esteem.

One cannot avoid noticing a marked tendency by even some of the *leaders* of the federal tribes to refuse to acknowledge the credibility of any non federally recognized individual or tribe. While this attitude is insensitive, there are some obvious reasons for it.

Retaining tribal sovereignty is a constant uphill battle for tribal managers and maintaining even minimal tribal services with drastically reduced, federally administered budgets is a task that few of us would care to inherit. There is no way to escape the fact that the addition of even a single individual to tribal rolls amounts to a dilution of already meager available income or other treaty entitlements by exactly one more unit. Imagine multiplying this by scores of people - many of whom, given the opportunity, would exercise their right to share in benefits that they neither need nor deserve - and it is easier to comprehend the seemingly over-protective guardianship exhibited by leaders who have the awesome responsibility of insuring the welfare of their tribal members..

The advent of Indian Gaming laws which allow gambling on Indian trust lands (where states approve) and a resulting per-capita share of profits from these ventures has brought an influx of "new" Indians out of the woodwork seeking federal recognition. While there are certainly exceptions, the motivations of most of these are quite clear, and it's safe to say that *honoring their heritage* usually doesn't fit into the picture.

Both situations have understandably increased the apprehensions of native governments and caused them to question the legitimacy of those claiming native heritage, especially organized groups. Still, it is grossly unfair to stereotype everyone because of the selfish acts of a few, and it certainly seems out of character for such esteemed and capable Cherokee leaders as Principal Chiefs Joyce Dugan, Joe Byrd and John Ross. Perhaps the future will bring a realization of the error of this demeanor.

Ultimately, how well one is accepted and recognized by the majority of the Cherokee people depends on one simple word - *respect* - and the amount received will be in direct proportion to the amount given. Respect the people, their culture and traditions, and most of them will happily treat you as one of their own.

Contemporary Traditional Dress

Dressing in distinctive native attire at certain times is a great way to assert and exhibit ancestral pride, but it is very important to make these choices carefully, depending on the type of event you plan to attend. Cherokees scrutinize the dress of their own much more seriously than some people seem to realize, because they are so protective of image and desirous of accurate portrayals of their culture.

At inter-tribal festivals (pow-wows), it is not unusual to see Cherokee people dressed in a variety of Native American regalia (especially dancers), and there are differing views on the correctness of this. Some believe that Cherokees should always wear the traditional Cherokee dress of some period, regardless of the occasion, and they are quick to criticize those who do not strictly adhere to this. Others argue that the tribal dress they wear should be a matter of personal choice, so long as their selection is not offensive. This is likely to be a subject of continued discussion, so I'll interject my opinion for whatever it's worth.

There still are some pow-wows that are private, spiritual ceremonies which agreeably should be kept as pure and traditional as possible. But most pow-wows of today are publicized events open to the public that offer not only dance competitions among inter-tribal dancers, but also a trade place for vendors of every conceivable type of native merchandise. One day is often devoted exclusively to school age children and while they come to learn, they also want to participate and have fun. In these instances, I can see no harm in real Cherokees dressing in "anything Indian" so long as it accomplishes the task at hand - namely, getting the attention of children (and some adults for that matter). While they're standing in awe at whatever costume you are wearing and busily clicking photographs, it's very easy to say, *"My people of old really didn't wear clothes like these, but some Native Americans did, and we want you to have the opportunity to see them."*

If you doubt my philosophy here, try wearing a turban like Sequoyah is always pictured in (no offense intended) , and sit a few yards away from another Cherokee wearing a colorful, full-feathered headdress. Then compare the number of children who run excitedly in his direction with those who only look questionably at you in passing. You'll quickly see my point and although one could argue that in teaching situations, it's still best to be authentic, I maintain that first you have to get their attention. Explanations can come later. Besides, there are always plenty of people around in "correct" attire that you can point out as examples.

You'll also occasionally hear derogatory comments about white people -those with no native ancestry- dressing in Indian clothing and attending pow-wows. They are sometimes dubbed as "wannabees" or "white Indians," and often are even accused of trying to "steal" the spirituality of Native Americans. Here again, with the exceptions on exploitation noted earlier, I cannot disagree more. In this regard, Archie Sam, highly regarded Cherokee chief of the Medicine Springs Dance Ground near Tahlequah, Oklahoma summed it up nicely in parts of a speech he gave during a University of Oklahoma symposium on December 12, 1976:

"It was prophesied a long time ago that Indians would turn away from their heritage and ceremonies, and would become weak and lost. Still, when the prophets gazed into their crystal stones they saw in the far distant future a young generation rising who would appreciate the values of their heritage and ceremonies and would become a strong race of people. For this reason the traditional Cherokees are desperately trying to preserve their songs and dances.

It was further prophesied that when a non-Indian understands the Indian way of life and its value system and dresses like an Indian, the Indians will have found a true friend. So today, at our ceremonial grounds, we have many non-Indian friends. I personally remember when the non-Indian neighbors would come to the ceremonial grounds to play ball and dance. They were accepted as friends. They were true friends of the Indians."

What is considered the traditional dress of the Cherokee today? Ironically, according to the Cherokee National Historical Society, this question was not officially decided until about 1970 when a young lady named Virginia Stroud was chosen as *Miss Indian America*. Realizing that few dated paintings existed of Cherokee women during the 19th century, except for those of some means who wore the high fashion gowns of white society, a special committee was appointed by the leaders of the Western Cherokee Nation to study what Miss Stroud should wear to represent her people and heritage. A member of this committee, Mrs. Wynona Day , visited Cherokee, North Carolina searching for clues to traditional dress before the Trail of Tears. There, she came into possession of an old house dress which was over one hundred years old. This article was researched in old historical society documents and those in private collections and eventually authenticated as a model for the current Cherokee traditional ladies "*tear dress.*" [Note: pronounced as in "*tear* an ad from the paper."]

These garments are called tear dresses because in days of old, scissors were rare and all the pieces were actually torn from a single length of fabric. All parts are either squares or rectangles and the decorative trim is usually a band of contrasting, solid colored fabric fashioned so that the dress material can show through. The cutwork is usually some variation of simple diamond and square shapes. Today, they also are adorned with bands of colored ribbons.

This same committee confirmed that traditional jewelry was usually made from copper, although some gold and silver was used when available. Pearls, shells , and mother of pearl disks were often worn as pendants and medallions. These were ornately carved or decorated with pierced scroll work. Beadwork frequently adorned bags and belts with motifs of stylized vines, flowers and leaves.

Today, when referring to dresses, the term "tear" is also pronounced as in "trail of *tears*" and they are said to symbolize that infamous journey. Men wear "tear" or "ribbon" shirts fashioned very similar to the style of 19th Century white settlers, but they do not include the usual drop shoulders, gathers, gussets, ruffles or muslim cloth commonly worn by frontiersmen. They are highlighted with bands of colored ribbons and loose hanging ribbon streamers which replaced hide or hair fringes of old. Today, some say these symbolize the hidden "tears" of our ancestors who were forcibly removed from their native homeland and the real tears of helpless sympathizers as they watched the ruthless actions of their own government.

At any type of Cherokee function today, it can be said that "Tear" attire is the most commonly worn - and accepted - traditional dress. Several examples are shown in the following pages. They are relatively easy to make, but if your time is as limited as that of my family, you might want to acquire them commercially and the Native American source listed below does excellent and authentic work.

Ketukla Originals
P.O. Box 802
Millbrook, AL 36054
Phone 334-285-4722
or toll free
1-888-KETUKLA
(Brochure available)

Robin McClure, wife of author wearing traditional Cherokee Tear Dress by Ketukla.

The author's mother Marian Haley and fellow Cherokee tribal member David Bell in traditional tear shirt and dress.

Popular Cherokee River Cane flutist and recording artist Tommy Wildcat (Cherokee Nation West) in typical Cherokee tear shirt.

(Taken at the author's maternal family memorial marker, Skullbone, Tennessee).

Tuckaleeche Story, First Vice Chief, Cherokee Tribe of N.E. Alabama in traditional tear dress.

Time Walker Trilogy

© 1996 by Les Tate

{The first time I had the esteemed privilege of reading Les Tate's inspirational *"Time Walker Trilogy,"* I knew that it faithfully described a place and time to which I had been before and surely would someday return. It reminded me of that age old axiom, *"Those who have passed from this world die only when we, whom they loved, forget them."*

When I asked Les for permission to include his excellent work in *"Cherokee Proud,"* he modestly replied: *"Please feel to use it if you think it is appropriate. I have no family history of Native American ancestry, however I feel that it was a gift to me for some reason and was meant to be shared with others."*

One needs only to read the heartwarming words that follow to positively know that while this personable and talented gentleman may have not yet found any Native American Ancestors . . .they surely have found him}. . .

First Journey

**I hold a shard of pottery and a flint point,
Both made by ancestors of long ago;
People clothed in woven fiber,
Animal skin, and the feathers of an eagle.
The shard is etched and painted,
Perhaps the remnants of a forgotten legend.
The point is thin and finely made, ready for hafting.
Its keen edge is surprising, the balance good.
The color of the stone shows it came from far away.**

I close my eyes for a moment, thinking back,
Remembering old ones now gone.
The shard and the stone warm my hand.
I feel the gentle touch of an ancestors hand
Guiding my fingers across his-her ancient work.
It is not difficult to make. We will show you.
Grandfather has dark eyes,
Full of experience and wisdom.
Grandmother smiles at me, friendly and warm.
Welcome. Sit by the fire. Share our food.
It is a good life, we have much.
I need to learn much.
Smell the grass and trees,
The water and smoke.
Hear the children, animals, insects, and wind.
Feel with more than touch.
See with more than eyes.
Learn and understand with your mind and heart.
I need to learn more.
We will teach you, but that is enough for now.
It is better to fully understand a few words
Than half understand many words.
May I sit by your fire again?
I will bring a story about tomorrow.
Will you tell me, remind me, of things forgotten?

Second Journey

Tonight we sing the old songs, remembering.
The flute is like the wind,
The drums like distant thunder,

Like buffalo on the prairie.
Voices blend together in song,
A blanket woven from eons of existence.
Smoke rises from the campfire into the sky.
This gathering is good,
Seeing old friends from distant homes,
Dancing to the chant and the drum.
But the ride here was long and I am tired.
I close my eyes and listen to the breeze
Whispering about the Old Ones.
The spring wind blows across the hill
Warming my spirit.
I think back to my childhood
When we made the long trek to this place
Where the grass is green and the water cool.
Father Sun now watches the corn tassel.
An eagle circles overhead.
It is a good sign.
My husband and son will return soon
From their journey to trade for flaking stone,
For shell and an eagle pipe.
I continue working on the leather pouch
My son will wear at the dance.
The white buffalo looks almost real,
Like the one I saw in my youth.
A cloud covers the face of Father Sun,
The shadow passing over me.
As the sky darkens, I close my eyes,
Remembering the gathering last year,
Old friends returning with new stories
To pass on to our children.
The wind as it moves through the trees
Is like the voices of the People singing as one.

The end of the chant sounds.
I open my eyes and rise.
Tomorrow I will dance again
Wearing the white buffalo pouch
Inherited from my great-grandfather,
Made by his great-grandmother.
As I walk toward our tent,
The night owl calls.
Time to dream.

Third Journey

I stand before the mountain
Gazing at images scratched into the stone,
Colored by traces of soot and dyes.
The Old Ones left this record
To be read and remembered
By others who would come after.
I reach out, gently touching the curves and lines,
Feeling with curious fingers,
Wondering who stood here before,
The painter of life, of time.
I slowly pull my hand away,
My fingers are stained
By the colors of fresh paints
Prepared from the plants and the earth.
Beside me stands a man,
Tall, bronze, and bare-chested,
Painting this years story upon the mountain.
I gaze at some of the old images,
Remembering the voice of my grandfather

Telling the tales and legends of long ago.
I give the painter another bowl, another color.
Below is our village,
The smoke of the fire and the sounds of life
Rise on the wind to the Great Spirit.
The People prepare for the celebration
of harvest,
Thankful for Mother Earth and Father Sun,
For full bellies and children who laugh,
For the gathering, the song, and the dance.
The drawing is finished, another year recorded
We silently gather the brushes and paints,
Then together start down the trail,
We stop and turn to look once again
At the many drawings on this monument,
The history of the People in a sacred place.
The man turns his head and speaks,
His eyes on me as one well trusted,
His voice familiar and reassuring,
Are you ready, my brother?
I nod and we turn again to the trail.
The wind stirs my hair,
The sound of a voice lingering in my mind,
Perhaps it was merely the wind
Playing among the rocks.
I gaze at the stone wall before me
At ancient paintings and petroglyphs.
The watchful spirits of my relatives surround
me.
I am honored to be one in a long line
That reaches from ancient past to distant
future.
The wind stirs again,
Bringing the smell of wood smoke

And the voices of family and friends.
I remember and I understand;
Tonight I live again.

Three generations of the well-known Wildcat Family (Cherokee Nation West) perform an educational demonstration Stomp Dance.

About the Author...

Tony Mack McClure, a native Tennessean, is a mixed-blood Cherokee maternal descendant of Lucy Briant (Bryant) listed as a Cherokee reservee on the 1817 Reservation roll in Northern Georgia. His paternal Cherokee ancestors (McClure) were from Porum, Oklahoma (Indian Territories Cherokee Nation West).

Tony has been the producer/director of ***Bill Dance Outdoors,*** the nation's highest rated outdoors-oriented television series for more than 25 years. The program airs twice each weekend, January through September on *The Nashville Network.* An avid writer, Tony's work has appeared in numerous magazines and more than 250 newspapers; on all four television networks and major cable systems.

He is a certified member of the ***Native American Journalists Association,*** committeeman for the ***Tennessee Chapter of the National Trail of Tears Association***, and frequent speaker on Cherokee history and ancestry before social, civic and student groups.

And now, my grandmother,
the job is done . . .
So hear me - no more tears!
Once again, the rays of a warm and welcome sun
shine brightly over Chu-nan-nee,
burning the haze away.
The eagle is back,
soaring high and free.
And the music of the wind in your mountain valley
always reaches crescendo.

Pass It On!

Additional copies of this book can be purchased from the address below for $13.95 plus $3 shipping and handling. If you purchase a copy that you intend to personally contribute to a library or educational Institution, please advise us of the name and address to avoid duplications.

CHUNANNEE BOOKS
4040 Boothe Road
Somerville, Tennessee 38068

Please send me the following book(s). My check or money order for total amount shown is enclosed.

_____Copies of "CHEROKEE PROUD: A GUIDE FOR TRACING AND HONORING YOUR CHEROKEE ANCESTORS"(paperback) at $13.95 plus $3 shipping and handling.

$________________ Total Amount Enclosed.

Name ____
Address ______________________________________
City ____
State ____________ Zip ______________________

(Please Note: United Parcel Service will not deliver to P.O.Boxes)

*I plan to contribute a copy of this publication to the following: ______________________________________